The Book of Buddha

The Book of
Buddha

ARUNDHATHI SUBRAMANIAM

PENGUIN
ANANDA

An imprint of Penguin Random House

PENGUIN ANANDA

USA | Canada | UK | Ireland | Australia
New Zealand | India | South Africa | China | Singapore

Penguin Ananda is part of the Penguin Random House group of companies
whose addresses can be found at global.penguinrandomhouse.com

Published by Penguin Random House India Pvt. Ltd
4th Floor, Capital Tower 1, MG Road,
Gurugram 122 002, Haryana, India

Penguin
Random House
India

First published in Viking by Penguin Books India 2005
Published in Penguin Books 2009
Published in Penguin Ananda 2012

10 9 8 7 6 5 4 3 2

ISBN 9780143419969

Typeset in Sabon by Mantra Virtual Services, New Delhi

Printed at Manipal Technologies Limited, India

www.penguin.co.in

MIX
Paper | Supporting
responsible forestry
FSC® C043100

This is a legitimate digitally printed version of the book and therefore might not
have certain extra finishing on the cover.

Contents

Contents

Preface

I think I was five, and in my uncle's house, when it first registered—an impassive, somewhat weathered, limestone image, in the archetypal Gandhara style. It was a face of extraordinary tranquility. A face that presented a stark contrast to the densely populated pantheon of Hindu gods that dominated my childhood devotional landscape.

The gods I knew in my mother's puja room were a vibrant bunch, captured in states of perpetual animation: the dancing Nataraja, the playful Krishna, the devoted Hanuman, the benign Ganapati. Arrestingly idiosyncratic personalities in their own right, all of them. But somehow they seemed to be busy folk, preoccupied with activities of an external kind. None of them exuded the air of untroubled interiority that this limestone figure did.

I mulled over the image in the inarticulate manner of a five-year-old. What was he thinking about? Was he never angry? Never sad? Above all, never bored? Was it actually possible to be so immersed in some world inside the self?

And so, without knowing it, my fascination with the Buddha had begun.

The Amar Chitra Katha comic that I stumbled on

sometime later, offered a life-story, but of a schematic sort. It only endorsed the impression I already had—of a compelling but puzzling inwardness. In my teens, I rediscovered the Buddha through other channels: through S. Radhakrishnan and Hermann Hesse, Alan Watts and Christmas Humphreys. He remained an inspirational figure, but for other reasons. He appealed now as the heroic solitary seeker who blazed his own trail; the man who asked the same questions that I did but dared to devote his entire life to addressing them.

But most importantly, here was a sage who didn't patronize me. He didn't tell me that he belonged to the hallowed echelons of the spiritual elect. He didn't smile down beatifically from some rarefied stratosphere. Here was someone who didn't demand weak-kneed veneration. He seemed to be comfortable with equality. We could be friends, I thought (with some impunity, forgivable perhaps in a seventeen-year-old). If you met him on the road, went the famous Zen epigram (that I, like many others, found so enticing), kill him. Here at last, I felt, was someone who spoke my language.

More than a decade-and-a-half later, I find that he still speaks it. I have approached him time and again— not as a student of philosophy or history, but as a seeker, with a seeker's mix of curiosity and desperation. He seldom lets me down. Few seem to have articulated the human predicament with quite the same degree of lucidity, psychological acuity and unsentimental precision. And it is as a seeker—not as a scholar—that I approach him once again in this book.* What empowered me in what often seemed like a formidable enterprise was the man himself and his own staunch refusal to turn the existential journey into a matter for experts and cardholders.

Life is dukkha, suffering, he says in a formulation that strikes you each time you read it with its chilling incontrovertibility. But it is by no means a no-exit situation. There is a way out, he reminds you, instantly challenging any notion you might begin to nurse about a creed of joyless pessimism. And here is a way that is entirely in keeping with the spiritual democrat who charted it—a way open to all. A way that does not require cosmic revelation or sacerdotal intercession. A way to a truth that is neither exclusive nor doctrinaire. A truth that is available to all who care to reach for it; a truth that knows no custodian or arbiter—nor even (and this is the great paradox of his powerful insight), a person to comprehend it.

And each time I find myself in a state of corrosive self-doubt—each time it seems like an act of hubris to hope for any transformation in my understanding of myself or the world—his generous invitation to all humanity comes to mind yet again: 'Look within, *you* are the Buddha.'

---

* For Pali and Sanskrit terms, which are not necessarily equivalent, I have chosen, in most cases, the version more familiar to readers.

Introduction

'*You are like a withered leaf, waiting for the messenger of death. You are about to go on a long journey, but you are so unprepared. Light the lamp within; strive hard to attain wisdom. Become pure and innocent, and live in the world of light.*' (Chapter 18, Dhammapada)

More than 2500 years ago, a thirty-five-year-old man had an insight under a peepul tree in north-eastern India. The insight was to create major shifts along the internal fault lines of generations of humanity for centuries to come. Today, over 300 million people across the globe consider themselves beneficiaries of that insight, and believe that it has irrevocably marked their spiritual commitment and identity.

Today, I gaze at my flickering computer screen on a rainy July evening and I wonder at this man, my contemporary in another age. A man whose fevered meaning-of-life questions ceased one night under a full moon in May. How did they cease, even while mine show no signs of abating? Who was this man who still remains such a vital figure for the modern-day questor? How did he arrive at the realization (brilliantly encapsulated by the scholar Buddhaghosha), the one that still boggles our minds, even while we have a subliminal hunch of its veracity: 'Suffering alone exists, but none who suffer; the deed there is, but no doer thereof; Nirvana there is, but no one seeking it; the Path there is, but none who travel it'?

In a world that grudgingly grants people their fifteen minutes in the spotlight, how does he continue to command attention across barriers of culture and chronology? How do we explain his unflagging shelf life, his dogged relevance to our lives?

The pop version of the chronicle of his life has something to do with it, of course. The saga follows all the conventions of the sure-fire page-turner: Rich Kid turns Renunciant in a spellbinding riches-to-rags-to-riches success story (even if the final success can't quite be measured in material terms).

But this is not just a feel-good story either. For the Buddha does not always offer succour even when we desperately feel we need it. Instead, he seems to frequently offer unsettling home truths. When Krisha Gautami approaches him, wild-eyed and disconsolate, lamenting the death of her child, he offers no token words of solace to allay her grief. Nor does he perform a miracle and bring the child back from the dead. He tells her, instead, to go around the village and bring a mustard seed from a home that hasn't experienced death. When Krisha Gautami is unable to find any such household, she has already moved from a personal grief to a deeper understanding of the endemic nature of human suffering.

Could the Buddha have done it another way, I've often wondered. Surely he could have clucked over her a bit, shown more overt compassion? Perhaps. But his response in this probably apocryphal story remains typical of his strategy as a teacher, and eventually it is for this very reason that we trust him. It's futile to expect chicken soup for the soul from a man who leaves us uncertain about the very existence of the soul! What we can expect from the Buddha instead is searing insight, astringent clarity, and a wisdom we recognize even before we fully apprehend it.

Why does the Buddha still speak to us?

For one, I suspect it's because he seems to ask the same questions that we ask. His life-story reveals him initially as the tormented seeker, the man who cannot be satisfied with the placebos and palliatives with which the status quo habitually silences its interrogators. Questions about human suffering, the fleeting nature of pleasure, the impermanence of all that we cherish. He seems to ask these questions with the same urgency and anguish as the rest of us.

Besides, it is difficult not to think of him every time we are confronted with suffering. When we watch loved ones succumb to the torturous indignities of terminal disease or old age. When we wake at 3 a.m. with the primal dread of our own dissolution. When we rise daily to confront a world that we know is far from innocent: a world inured to genocide, starvation death and female infanticide, a world that compels us to face time and again that even if our hands aren't as bloody, our minds are as insatiably acquisitive and violent as the next person's. At such times, one remembers him suddenly as the man who's been there, seen that. This is the seasoned sleuth who plunged into the roiling tangle of the deepest layers of human consciousness and returned to tell us that there was a way out. That it is possible for all of us to learn the ancient alchemy of transforming adversity into freedom, brokenness into wholeness, the sound and fury of the gibbering mind into flawless peace. His is a language that still seems to address the fragmentation, the alienation, the sense of moral collapse and spiritual desiccation that make up the modern experience.

On other occasions, the memory of the Buddha creeps up on us during an unplanned interstice in the frantic business of life. We suddenly become aware of the sense of unease and Kierkegaardian dread that underlies our lives, the niggling feeling of not being where we are meant to be. Contemporary spiritual master, Eckhart Tolle, calls it 'the background static of perpetual discontent' that most human beings live with and often consider normal.

And even if we happen to be among those who prefer to deal with problems as they arise, and not fret about the imponderables, it's difficult not to be startled into a moment's unwitting attention when we stumble on those lines of the Buddha: 'If people, doomed to undergo old age, illness and death, are carefree in their enjoyment with others who are in the same position, they behave like birds and beasts . . . By contrast, I become frightened and greatly alarmed when I reflect on the dangers of old age, death and disease. I find neither peace nor contentment, and enjoyment is quite out of the question, for the world looks to me as if ablaze with an all-consuming fire.'

These words are not simply part of the hortatory rhetoric of a finger-wagging moralist. The image of the all-consuming fire comes surely from the mind of the mystic poet—the man who sees what each of us sees and puts it into words before we do. He only confirms our deepest gut feeling. The Buddha speaks to us because he tells us what we know intuitively to be true.

At the same time, he does not ask you to drown your rational mind either. There is nothing anti-intellectual about the Buddha's stance. It is, in fact, difficult to find someone who affirms the powers of insight and discernment, instinct and reason, with quite the same even-handedness. I believe he speaks to us because he does not tell us suffering is an illusion, or that it's good for our souls. He does not ask us to believe in a pain-free world. He does not ask for the impossible. He does not ask us to lay aside a belief system and adopt another. He does not ask for our unswerving obedience or any extravagant act of undying faith. He does not ask for blind faith in scripture, uncritical allegiance to tradition, or self-abnegating devotion to a master. He simply never stretches the limits of our credulity. If his words challenged a highly ascriptive caste-bound society in his day, they are equally compelling for a contemporary world where a progressively fascist mindset seeks security over freedom, the ghetto over the community.

All the Buddha does ask of the seeker is a wholehearted inner commitment to the path to liberation. In a direct challenge to the Brahmin hegemony of his day, he told his listeners on multiple occasions that his teaching could be directly experienced by anyone willing to put in the necessary application. He refused to entertain the possibility of having his vernacular doctrine translated into the refined cadences of classical Sanskrit verse. He was equally emphatic about not introducing any esoteric–exoteric divide into his teaching. As he told his senior disciple, Ananda, on his deathbed: 'The Law that I have taught has no secret and public versions: there is no "teacher's closed fist" about good things here.' Time and again one finds proof of the egalitarian nature of his pedagogic practice. It is an approach that still induces awe when one thinks of the insidious ways in which notions of hierarchy and privilege perpetuate themselves in our world.

Why does the Buddha speak to us? Because the Path he urges us to follow does not require us to be narrow or sectarian, exclusivist or dogmatic. No wonder then that Buddhism has often been termed 'a science of the mind' rather than a religion. To be a Buddhist is to take refuge in the three supreme realities: the Buddha; the Dharma; and the Sangha. None of these need be interpreted in any prescriptive way. The Buddha refers to the prince of Kapilavastu who found the path to everlasting peace. But it also refers to all those figures in diverse places and moments in history that stumbled upon 'the ancient trail'. Mahayana Buddhism tells us, in fact, that there are several Buddhas who live in all places and at all times.

The Dharma refers to the doctrine of the Buddha, but again does not enjoin a literal understanding of any kind. To take refuge in the Dharma is to take refuge simply in the immutable law of mutability, in the way things are, the intrinsic harmony of the undivided mind, the robust commonsensical advice ('In walking, just walk. In sitting, just sit. Above all, don't wobble') of the Zen Buddhist.

Finally, the Sangha, even while it refers to the order of monks and nuns established by the Buddha, also connotes in a truly hospitable sense a community of seekers across cultures and faiths that dedicates itself to finding a still point in a turning world.

To be a Buddhist, in the broad sense of the term, then, is not to acquire a new system of beliefs and scriptural verities, but to let go of every subtle kind of conceptual idolatry. It is to learn to accept flux rather than petrify experience into a structure of illusory permanence; figuratively speaking, not to seek comfort in capital letters but to learn to live in lower case. The path to nirvana is about learning to travel light, to strip away the endless superfluities of opinion, philosophy, ideology and prejudice with which we swaddle ourselves out of fear of our own vulnerability. It is to divest ourselves of the accretions of identity we've acquired out of our habitual oscillation between attachment and aversion, craving and disgust.

Perhaps what makes the modern seeker trust this wisdom is its inherent disavowal of anything cultist. The Buddha does not ask you to follow him, the historic trailblazer. He doesn't ask you to cling to a new saviour, but asks everyone 'to be lamps unto yourselves. Betake yourselves to no external refuge. Look not for refuge to anyone beside yourself. Hold fast to the Truth as to a lamp.' Yes, he is a historically particular phenomenon, but more important than himself, as he was at pains to point out, is the Path—one that leads you beyond history and the world of phenomena.

And why yet another book on the life of a much-documented figure?

Because the Buddha's relevance shows no signs of diminishing. Because retelling is a way of remembering, revisiting, reclaiming—a pilgrimage on the page. And finally, a Zen answer that's difficult to resist: Because.

Siddhartha, the Seeker

'Better than ruling this world, better than attaining the realm of the gods, better than being lord of all the worlds, is one step taken on the path to nirvana.' (Chapter 13, Dhammapada)

It is not easy to tease fact out of the mists of myth and hagiography that cling to the life of the Buddha. While this account does seek to locate some kernel of historical probability in the retelling of this well-worn tale, it does not intend to offer a narrative pasteurized of all legend either. For fables, however fantastic, often point to truths that elude obsessively factual chronicles.

The aim in the following story is not to deify the Buddha, nor is it to engage in some Procrustean downsizing simply in order to turn him into a comfortably identifiable figure. The idea is to explore the life of an exceptional but enigmatic human being—to wonder at, rather than hope to encompass; to arrive at a version rather than the definitive story of his life and times. There seems to be some factual basis to the biography of the Buddha that we have inherited, but this is inseparable from the richly symbolic narratives that also characterize the ancient records. The biographies were in any case compiled after his death and orally transmitted for centuries. Further overlaid by the interpolations and embellishments of centuries of raconteurs, they may not entirely satisfy a penchant for consistency or intimate detail. But they do offer us the arresting silhouette of a man, inflected at times with unexpected shades and contours. To read about the Buddha is to enter the realm where the frontiers between fact and fiction fade. The result is a figure that is both man and metaphor.

The tale of Siddhartha Gautama—later the Buddha—takes us back to a day in the month of May, six centuries before the Christian era. His mother, Maya, was on her way from her marital abode in Kapilavastu, in the Himalayan foothills, to her parental home in Devadaha for her delivery. The birth, probably brought on prematurely by a bumpy ride in a cart, took place under a sal tree in the village of Lumbini, and with no medical assistance. It is perhaps appropriate that the birth of the world's greatest spiritual democrat was a quiet affair, entirely shorn of royal pomp and ceremony.

Some accounts, however, inform us that it was by no means an unremarkable event, and a need for poetic justice may make us warm to this view. According to the Pali canonists, 'when the Bodhisattva had passed away from the Heaven of the Contented and entered his mother's womb, a great measureless light surpassing the splendour of the gods appeared in the world'. Maya herself, in accordance with the mythic depictions of great mother-figures, is said to have been purified of all sensual desire and was free of fatigue and affliction during the pregnancy.

According to legend, ten lunar months after conception, on her way to her parent's home, Maya paused for a respite in the pleasure grove of Lumbini, and was carried to the foot of a sal tree. She stretched out a hand to seize a branch, but the branch itself stooped down to come within her grasp. At this point, she was suddenly seized with birth pangs, whereupon her attendants set up a curtain for her to offer her privacy. Still clutching the branch, even as she was standing, Maya gave birth to the child who was to grow up and transform the spiritual destiny of millions.

The canon proceeds to relate how the child was received on a golden net, miraculously provided by the gods. Though the child was unstained by the process of birth, two ritual streams of water were poured from the sky by divine dispensation to cleanse the mother and child. Physically exquisite in every respect because of his virtuous karma in previous lives, Siddhartha's body bore the thirty-two major marks and eighty minor marks that were signs of future greatness. Immediately after birth, the infant took seven steps and proclaimed with a lion's roar, 'I am the Ruler of the world'. According to another account, he advanced east and declared, 'I will reach the highest Nirvana'; then south and stated, 'I will be the first of all creatures'; then west and said, 'This will be my last birth'; and finally north, stating, 'I will cross the ocean of existence'.

At that moment, all living beings in all the realms of existence thrilled with pleasure; musical instruments, both celestial and earthly, sounded without being touched; trees of all seasons burst into blossom; and a gentle breeze began to waft, bearing perfumes of every kind from the country of the gods. Even if this legend does seem a trifle florid, it offers a more comforting alternative to the gritty tale of an unattended childbirth in the Himalayan wilderness.

Siddhartha's family belonged to the ruling aristocracy of a small republic nestled in the southern foothills of the Himalayas, an ancient terrain now divided by the Indo-Nepal border. Historians generally consider his date of birth to be 563 BCE, although it is possible that this is off the mark by five or nine years. While not quite the heir of a great Indian monarch that legend has often painted him to be, there is no denying that Siddhartha was born into a life of privilege. His father, Shuddhodana, was the Kshatriya ruler of the clan of the Shakyas, and governed his small republic from the capital of Kapilavastu.

The Shakyan republic was one of the several oligarchic republics in the Central Gangetic plain. The others included the republics of the Mallas, the Lichhavis, and the Videhas, each of which was ruled by an elected Kshatriya governor. The political landscape of the time was further defined by four kingdoms—

Kosala (north of the Ganga with its capital of Shravasti); Vamsa (south-west of Kosala with its capital of Kosambi); Avanti (south of the Ganga with its capitals of Ujjaini and Mahishmati), and Magadha (to the east of Avanti, with its capital of Rajagriha). There were also a number of tribes in the area, such as the Koliyas, the Moriyas and the Kalamas, ruled by appointed governors who were not necessarily Kshatriyas. Apart from the odd dispute over irrigation and pasture rights, the various domains with their distinct political systems seem to have maintained a general spirit of accord and amity.

Attempts to historically recreate the ground realities of the Shakyan republic, based on Chinese traveller Hieuan Tsang's account, have revealed that the region had a circumference of around 1880 kilometres, and an area of around 2000 square kilometres, much of which was forest land. There were ten cities, and a total population of around 1,80,000, of which 8000 people were probably located in Kapilavastu. The Shakyan republic was a vassal-state of the powerful kingdom of Kosala, and the elected oligarch probably paid taxes on a regular basis to his overlord in Shravasti. Nonetheless, within the confines of his republic, Shuddhodana was undoubtedly a man of importance, responsible for administration and the maintenance of law and order.

Shuddhodana had two wives: Maya and Mahaprajapati. Maya was his principal wife and the mother of Siddhartha. Mahaprajapati, a significant figure in Buddhist lore, was Maya's younger sister, later Siddhartha's foster mother, and later still the Buddha's first female disciple. She had two children: Nanda, a son (who was born a few days after Siddhartha), and Sundarinanda, a daughter.

After the delivery, Maya and her retinue returned to Kapilavastu. Weakened by the rigours of childbirth, she died seven days later. The care of Siddhartha was now entrusted to Mahaprajapati, who, by all accounts, proved to be a compassionate surrogate mother. According to some sources, she handed over her own son, Nanda, to a wet nurse, and devoted herself exclusively to the motherless child.

Three days after the birth, Asita, an old Brahmin seer and close family friend who had now retired to lead a hermit's life in the Himalayas, was invited to inspect the child. The sage was capable, it is said, of the extraordinary feat of looking forty lifetimes into the past and the future. This is the first dramatic event in the life of Siddhartha. One can imagine the grizzled soothsayer agreeing to pay a courtesy call on the ruler, but suddenly finding himself dumbfounded when confronted by the most astounding case history of his entire lifetime. 'This child will undoubtedly attain the summit of true knowledge, the supreme complete enlightenment,' prophesied the old astrologer when he had recovered.

'He will then set the wheel of Law in motion and take countless beings across the ocean of transmigration and establish them in the Immortal State.'

At this point, he was moved to tears for it struck him that he would not live to witness the extraordinary spiritual growth of the prince of Kapilavastu. Some days later, during the naming ceremony, several Brahmin priests affirmed Asita's prediction, proclaiming that the son of Shuddhodana would grow to become the ruler of a mighty spiritual or political empire. These predictions obviously elated Shuddhodana.

There is little information in the scriptures about Siddhartha's early years, although later literature offers several anecdotes about this period. Clearly, the tale of the prince reared in hothouse isolation, in the luxurious palace of Sans Souci, is something of a construct. Siddhartha's childhood of relative seclusion probably had something to do with a privileged upbringing, as well as the quasi-political autonomy of the Shakyan republic. Even his 'palace' is likely in actual fact (as H.W. Schumann, author of 'The Historical Buddha', points out) to have been no more than a multi-storey brick construction, built on a slight elevation, distinct from the clay, bamboo and reed huts that belonged to the rest of the populace.

However, it is entirely believable that Shuddhodana was concerned enough about his son to want to insulate him as much as possible from the grimmer realities of the outside world. This could have been partly prompted by the parental fear of losing him to a spiritual life. It could also have been partly fuelled by Siddhartha's own sensitive and brooding temperament, which was regarded as not quite a fitting personality profile for the son of a ruler. Hence, Shuddhodana's desire to ensure that his son was offered all the material comforts at his command. The young prince evidently knew the good life. He had access to the best sandalwood and cloth from Varanasi. He was surrounded by lotus ponds with blue, red and white blossoms, and had different sleeping quarters for the three seasons. In his post-marital monsoon abode, according to one somewhat hedonistic account, he was actually attended by all-female minstrels! A white parasol was ritually held over him to protect him from the cold, heat and dust. Even his servants had a regular diet of full-grained rice and meat. It was, in words attributed to Siddhartha himself, 'a spoilt, very spoilt life'.

He seems to have grown up into an intelligent, attractive and accomplished young man. The canon frequently eulogizes his appearance in his later years as a Buddha. Even though some of these effusions may have simply been in keeping with the traditional veneration of a spiritual icon, the many reiterations of his height and carriage, and the golden lustre of his complexion, probably had some basis in reality. I visualize the young Siddhartha as a slender man, of above-average height, radiant complexion, bright-eyed, but with a decidedly inward gaze. The artistic imagination of painters and sculptors has, of course, dwelt extensively on his appearance after his enlightenment. On seeing the famous statue of the 'Buddha with Sapphire Eyes' in Sri Lanka, the Russian mystic P.D. Ouspensky wrote: 'His face was neither cold nor indifferent. On the other hand it would be quite wrong to say that it expressed warmth or sympathy or compassion . . . No, it was a human face, yet at the same time a face which men do not happen to have. I felt that all the words I could command would be wrong if applied to the expression of this face. I can only say that here was *understanding*.'

And yet, the handsome young patrician did not grow up to be a pampered child. What saved him from that fate was obviously his temperament—an exploratory mind and an unconventional spirit that could not be satisfied with the certitudes of received wisdom. He was perhaps too introverted to be a flagrant rebel, but he was also far too intellectually subversive for parental comfort. It is also clear that while he was trained in riding, archery, fencing, wrestling and chariot-driving, as befitted his Kshatriya upbringing, he was decidedly uninspired by martial pursuits.

Siddhartha's account of his early dissatisfaction with the worldly life reaches across the centuries and moves one even today with its quiet ring of authenticity:

'And, monks, in the midst of that happy life the thought came to me: Truly, the simple worldling, who is himself subject to old age, is disgusted when he sees an old man. But I too am subject to old age and cannot escape it. At this thought, monks, all delight in my youth left me.

'Truly, the simple worldling, who is himself subject to disease, is disgusted when he sees a sick man. But I too am subject to disease and cannot escape it. At this thought, monks, all delight in my health left me.

'Truly, the simple worldling, who is himself subject to death, is disgusted when he sees a dead man. But I too am subject to death and cannot escape it. At this thought, monks, all delight in my life left me.'

One of the incidents of his early life that one suspects is historically true (simply because there is nothing intrinsically dramatic about it) is that of his spontaneous meditation under a rose-apple tree during the annual ploughing ceremony. Sitting in the cool shade of the tree, Siddhartha lazily watched his father perform the ritual act of ploughing the field that formally inaugurated the sowing season. Suddenly the young man found himself entering a state of deep unpremeditated absorption, a state of withdrawal accompanied by tranquility and an inexplicable happiness. Although Siddhartha did not know it at the time, this was a significant precursor to his great spiritual awakening. It also left a lasting enough impression for him to recall it in later years.

According to a more picturesque version of the same incident, 'as he saw the young grass torn up and scattered by the plough, and . . . the insects that had been killed, (Siddhartha) was overcome by a deep sorrow, as though he had witnessed a massacre of his own people'. As a result, 'this noblest among men was filled with the most profound compassion' and embarked for the very first time on a contemplation of universal suffering. Much later, towards dusk, when Shuddhodana sent attendants to look for his son, they found him in deep meditation under the tree. There is a lyrical appropriateness to the miracle that is said to have occurred: 'The sun was now sinking towards the horizon, but the shadow of the rose-apple tree had not moved, and continued to protect the divine youth.'

A well-known legend recounts how the gentle Siddhartha rescued and nursed a bird that had been shot down by his more martial cousin, Devadatta (who recurs in the Buddha's biography in later years). Insisting that the bird belonged to him, a truculent Devadatta appealed to the king: 'I shot the bird, it is rightfully mine.' But none could counter Siddhartha's quiet logic: 'To whom should any creature belong: to he who tries to kill it or to he who saves its life?'

When Siddhartha turned sixteen, his parents arranged for his marriage with Yashodhara, the sixteen-year-old daughter of the Shakya Dandapani. They must have hoped that it would have some impact on his unworldly bent of mind. They were probably not disappointed. There is evidence enough to suggest that the couple were attracted to each other. The vehemence of the Buddha's later warnings to his disciples to beware the snare of female charms suggests that he knew only too well how overpowering the chemistry of the man–woman relationship can be. While he was obviously in love with his wife, the nagging sense that he was meant for another destiny did not leave him. According to one account, when he laid his head against Yashodhara's breast and lapsed into a state of sensual slumber, he would often sit up with a start of alarm and cry, 'My world! O world! I hear, I know, I come.'

The metaphysical landscape in Siddhartha's day was by no means an unsophisticated one. To understand his own choices, it is useful to have some idea of the highly evolved philosophical temper of his times. The spiritual tradition of the Vedas had become increasingly associated with social orthodoxy and exclusivist Brahmanism, and the Vedic sacrificial cult had degenerated into a tired ritualistic affair. The wisdom of the Upanishads with its philosophical basis of mystic non-dualism—the unity of the Atman and the Brahman—

was already in existence. (Five of the Upanishads were extant in the pre-Buddhist age.) However, the inspired originality of this doctrine had been gradually appropriated by the Brahmin ritualists, and the revolutionary 'open secret' of this whispered doctrine was now appended to the Vedic canon as the Vedanta, the culmination of the Vedas.

Unsurprisingly, there was a growing tribe of spiritual aspirants that defined itself against the rigidity of tradition by rejecting the varied guises of Brahmin elitism. This seeker was essentially a homeless man, a wayfarer and alms-gatherer, who renounced conventional social relationships to wander the world in search of spiritual illumination. He was known as the parivrajaka when he was a Brahmin, and a shramana when he was from any of the other castes. The shramanas did not constitute a homogeneous category in terms of ideology or practice. The ultimate goal was deliverance, but the approaches were varied, ranging from philosophical idealism to nihilism, from rabid iconoclasm to the gentler non-conformity of unfettered personal quest.

There were the materialists (the Lokayatas or Charvakas) who were contemptuous of all doctrines of salvation, and stoutly averred that whatever cannot be perceived by the senses does not exist. These were the sceptics and hedonists whose rich repertoire of irreverent jibes checked the unworldly excesses of the eternalist schools of thought. Then there were Tapasvins, or ascetics, who regarded the purification of the body through flagellation and rigorous penance as the means to emancipation. Among the many severe practices of self-mortification were fasting, taking a vow of silence, mutilating the body, emulating the life of a cow or dog, abstaining from sleep, lying on a bed of thorns, assuming difficult postures, such as standing in water, or curtailing the movement of the body in drastic ways.

Another genre of heterodox spiritual seeker was the determinist (Ajivaka) who held that everything, including salvation, was predetermined. Yet another category was the individual seeker, impatient with the confines of tradition, but flexible enough to experiment with various approaches, by spending his time with gurus of diverse persuasions. And there was also the universal figure of the freethinking drifter, with no quest at all, who probably preferred a life of social independence, without the burdensome responsibilities of a householder.

Lively seminars between groups of different persuasions were held regularly in the outskirts of villages and towns, usually in groves. The young Shakyan, Siddhartha, must have been a bystander at many of these heated metaphysical disputes. These obviously left a deep impression on him.

Desiring a life of political empire for his son, Shuddhodana did his best to circumscribe Siddhartha's activities within the elite circles of the ruling aristocracy. But as the young man matured, these efforts were doomed to failure. Siddhartha's growing engagement with his environment is symbolized in the famous story *The Four Signs*. While it is clearly not intended for literal interpretation, this tale from the *Nidanakatha* (authored several centuries after the Buddha's time) has become the definitive parable of the 'turning point' in Siddhartha's spiritual trajectory. On a surreptitious foray into the outside world with his faithful horse, Kanthaka, and his loyal charioteer, Channa, Siddhartha came upon the first of his life-transforming sights: an old man, bent, shivering and decrepit, with grey hair and decaying teeth. On a second journey, he stumbled upon a diseased man. On yet another excursion, he saw a corpse.

Shaken out of the pervasive human delusion of immortality, young Siddhartha was now forced to confront the inevitability of pain, indignity and dissolution. His dramatic collisions with reality provoked those questions that have jolted every human being into moments of chilling disquiet at some point or the other: What is the meaning of this life if everything we hold precious is doomed to eventual extinction? How can we pretend that all is well with the world, when it so obviously isn't? Are we mere pawns in this cycle of birth, suffering and death? Who authored this absurdly unjust system? Have we no choice, no volition at all, except to submit to its whimsical diktats? To all his fevered queries, Siddhartha's companion, Channa, could only shake his head sadly and reply, 'Yes, Master, there is no escape. Old age, sickness, death—such is the lot of all men.'

A fourth encounter with a shramana catalysed the great departure. The calm that emanated from the mendicant's face convinced Siddhartha that there was an alternative—that it was possible to map out one's life differently, to choose a path other than one of bovine obedience to the socially prescribed blueprint. It was obviously a radical decision; it meant renouncing a family, a home, social status, prestige, a life of hereditary privilege. Besides, the life of the shramana came with no guarantees. It promised hardship but no certain nirvana, no unequivocal answer to the burning question of life and death. But it had now become clear to Siddhartha that the less-trodden path no longer represented one option among many. The seeker could not turn into a sanguine householder, even if he wanted to. There could be no going back.

And so dawned the day of what has come, in Buddhist lore, to be known as the Great Departure. Siddhartha was now twenty-nine years old. At nightfall, he asked for his horse, Kanthaka, to be bridled by

Channa. He then stole into his wife's chamber to bid her and his infant child a silent farewell. After thirteen years of childlessness, Yashodhara had just borne them a son, Rahula. The oil lamp went out as he entered the room, and since Yashodhara held her hand protectively over the child's head, it was impossible for Siddhartha to catch a last glimpse of his son. Neither could he touch him for fear of waking him. He took a long glance at the two sleeping figures, turned and left his home forever.

Siddhartha's silent leave-taking of his wife and son often reads like a cruel forsaking of two defenceless dependants. There is no easy way to rationalize this event. And yet, this act of domestic treachery proved later to have spiritual repercussions of world significance. Besides, the life of the homeless shramana was regarded as an honourable path in Siddhartha's time. To choose it was not an act of moral cowardice. There is also a poignancy in the account that suggests that it was by no means easy for the young husband and father to divest himself of these attachments.

And so Siddhartha left his parental abode in the dead of night, riding his stallion, and accompanied by the ever-faithful Channa. The east gate of the city, locked and guarded, is supposed to have opened miraculously for him, suggesting yet again the inevitability of this great act of renunciation. Siddhartha reached the river Anoma that night, where he cut off his hair and donned the robe of a shramana. There are varied accounts of this great adventure. Some say he surrendered his expensive garments to a woodcutter. Others tell us that he cut off his hair with his sword till it was 'two fingers in length', which, it is believed, is how it remained for the rest of his days. Still others say that he sent back his locks to his family as a memento. He also entrusted his beloved horse and ornaments to Channa, who brought them back to Kapilavastu. According to one legend, Kanthaka died of a broken heart after his master's departure and was immediately 'reborn as a god'.

However, in another, less sensational version, supposedly told in the Buddha's own voice, his intention to adopt the homeless life was not concealed from his family, or, at least, not from his parents. Shuddhodana and Mahaprajapati did their best to restrain him, but Siddhartha remained obdurate. It is possible that his parents had persuaded him to remain in the household until the birth of a grandson. This could explain why the marriage remained childless for thirteen years. Finally, on the birth of Rahula, Siddhartha's aspirations could be quelled no longer:

'When I was still a Bodhisattva, the thought came to me: "The household life, this place of impurity, is narrow—the shramana life is the free, open air. It is not easy for a householder to lead the perfected, utterly pure and perfect holy life. What if I were now to cut off my hair and beard, don yellow (shramana) robes, and go forth from the household into homelessness?"

'And I, being young, a youth with black hair, in the prime of my youth, in the first stage of manhood, cut off my hair and beard, although my father and (foster) mother opposed this and wept with tearful faces, donned the yellow robe and went forth from the household life into homelessness.'

Siddhartha spent the first week of his new life in a mango grove near the village of Anupiya, before wending his way towards the great city of Vaishali. One of the most famous spiritual quests in history was now underway.

The Long Journey Upstream

Siddhartha's first, formal spiritual apprenticeship was with Alara Kalama, a famous spiritual adept and teacher. It is here that Siddhartha was trained in the attainment of the State of Nothingness—a practice that the keen aspirant internalized in an amazingly short period of time. Kalama soon regarded his precocious pupil 'as equal to himself' and honoured him by offering him the position of fellow-leader of his order. However, Siddhartha was still dissatisfied. This was not nirvana, 'the unborn, unageing, unailing, deathless, sorrowless, undefiled supreme surcease of bondage', and he was unwilling to settle for less.

He then proceeded to Rajagriha, the capital of the Magadhan kingdom. It was on an alms-round that he was first spotted by King Bimbisara, who was struck by his distinguished appearance and guessed him to be of noble pedigree: 'of high-born warrior stock, one fit to grace a first-rate army'. The king accosted this young pilgrim and offered him a fortune, even the entire sovereignty of his kingdom. (While this seems unlikely, it does suggest the deep impression that Siddhartha made on the king.) However, the man who had already renounced a family and social position, with all their attendant comforts, had no qualms about refusing: 'I have not gone forth to seek sense pleasures. I have gone out to strive.' This encounter sowed the seeds of a lifelong respect and friendship between the two men.

It was probably in Rajagriha that Siddhartha became a pupil of Udraka Ramaputra, another master of renown. With admirable speed, the seeker attained an exalted state of absorption known as the State of Neither Perception nor Non-Perception. But he soon realized that he could not deceive himself: this law 'did not lead to dispassion, to fading of lust, to cessation, to peace, to direct knowledge, to enlightenment, to Nirvana'. He had become a virtuoso meditator but was still no closer to self-realization. Declining Ramaputra's generous offer to install him as the head of his order of monks, Siddhartha decided it was time to make another break. Spurning the lure of a secure, institutional position yet again, he moved on.

Wandering restlessly through the Magadhan country, the young mendicant arrived at an idyllic spot in a grove by a riverside at Uruvela. The picturesque beauty of the place and its proximity to a village that could serve as an alms-resort, recommended it as the ideal site for further practice.

Now dawned the most severe phase in Siddhartha's quest for enlightenment. A mounting frustration at the elusive nature of truth made him plunge into an uncompromising tryst with asceticism. Since self-denial was the practice enjoined by several teachers of the time (including his other great contemporary, Mahavira), the Buddha was later at pains to impress upon his following that he had practised every conceivable act of self-mortification, but to no avail. His account catalogues each step in graphic detail: 'Suppose, with my teeth clenched and my tongue pressed against the roof of my mouth, I beat down, constrain and crush my mind with my mind? Then, as a strong man might seize a weaker by the head or shoulders and beat him down, constrain him and crush him, so . . . I crushed my mind with my mind.' Perspiration coursed down his body as he relentlessly pursued this practice of self-subjugation. He was able to attain a state of 'unremitting mindfulness', but he eventually abandoned this strategy when he realized that his body was overwrought as a result of sheer fatigue.

His next step was to hold the in-breaths and out-breaths in his nose and mouth, and observe the result. At this point, the winds issuing from his ears produced a sound like 'a smith's bellows'. When he also stopped the breaths in his ears, violent winds racked his head, 'as if a strong man were splitting my head open with a sharp sword'. In a vivid series of images, he speaks of how agonizing pains racked his head 'as if a strong man were tightening a tough leather strap round my head as a head-band' and violent winds 'carved up my belly as a clever butcher or apprentice carves up an ox's belly with a sharp knife'. Then followed a burning sensation in the stomach 'as if a strong man had seized a weaker by both arms and were roasting him over a pit of live coals'.

His next step was to reduce his intake of food to a handful a day. As a result, he grew painfully emaciated. His 'limbs became like the joined segments of vine or bamboo stems . . . (his) backside became like a camel's hoof . . . (his) ribs jutted out as gaunt as the crazy rafters of an old roofless barn . . .' If he touched his stomach he encountered his own backbone; when he relieved himself, he fell over on his face on the spot; if he ever

'It is hard to obtain human birth, harder to live like a human being, harder still to understand the dharma, but hardest of all to attain nirvana.' (Chapter 14, Dhammapada)

What the Buddhist annals consider to be 'the greatest event in all human history' took place one full-moon night in the month of May in 544 BCE. Lest one conclude that every momentous incident in Buddhist history—including the birth of the founder—occurred in May, it is useful to remind ourselves that Japan, for instance, celebrates a December date. Historical exactitude of this kind was evidently not particularly important for the biographers.

Siddhartha was presumably thirty-five years old—a ravaged, weather-beaten, but by no means defeated, seeker—when he finally awoke to what the poet Rilke has called 'the news that is always arriving out of silence'. The relentless interrogator of spiritual verities now crossed the river (to use a common Buddhist image) and reached the other shore. From this moment on, he is no longer the tormented young man that readers recognize, however fleetingly, in themselves. As dawn broke on the eastern horizon, Siddhartha was transformed irreversibly into the Buddha, into Shakyamuni, the Sage of the Shakyas. The existential questor became the Enlightened One. The seeker turned into a sage.

In its inimitable metaphorical mode, the canon tells us that the event was presaged by five dreams on the preceding night. In the first dream, Siddhartha dreamt that the earth was his couch, the Himalayas his pillow, his left hand trailed the eastern ocean, his right hand plunged into the western ocean, and his feet touched the southern ocean. This was testimony to his enlightenment, his impending sovereignty over a vast spiritual empire. In the second dream, a creeper grew out of his navel, rose and touched the clouds, foretelling his discovery of a revolutionary doctrine. In the third dream, white worms with black heads crawled up his feet and covered his knees—a sign that a multitude of white-robed lay-followers would seek refuge in him. In the fourth dream, four birds of different colours from different quarters miraculously turned white as they alighted at his feet, symbolic of the four castes that would find equal access to salvation in his teaching. In the final dream, he walked through a huge mountain of dung but remained unsoiled—a vision of the future Awakened One who would live off the charity of others, but remain untainted by human desire and avarice.

Fortified by his meal and inspired by the auspicious omens, Siddhartha seated himself under a peepul, or ashwattha, tree that day in a state of profound resolution. Exhilarated by this new conviction, he was determined not to rise until he had attained the wisdom that had eluded him for years: 'Though my skin, my nerves and my bones should waste away and my life-blood dry, I will not leave this seat until I have attained Supreme Enlightenment.'

It was now clear to him that the flesh and spirit did not have to exist in a mutually antagonistic relationship. The instinctual had to be integrated, rather than denied, for liberation to be attained. This is an important moment in the story of Siddhartha, when we are offered an alternative to what is otherwise a typical male questor myth. It marks the moment of his realization that the spiritual journey cannot be an extension of a male imperialist project of conquest and domination. The woman seeker will probably also relate to the fact that it is in reclaiming a childhood memory—'re-membering' the past, as it were—that he resolves his impasse. When he recalls his spontaneous meditation under the rose-apple tree, Siddhartha realizes that spiritual maturity is not about mere transcendence, but about trusting one's inner resources as well.

Was Siddhartha's realization the result of personal volition or divine grace? Was it earned or bestowed? Was it determination or providential design that helped him achieve his end? The Buddhist tradition has stressed the vital role of personal effort, of committed unswerving practice, rather than passive faith. Rigour at this stage for Siddhartha did not mean arrogant mastery, but striving tirelessly to reach the point of dynamic responsiveness, a radical passivity. Faith and practice at this stage are probably no longer distinguishable— for practice itself can be interpreted as the process of aligning the individual will with cosmic law, of learning to collaborate with one's own destiny. In the mysterious realm of paradox that is the state of spiritual communion, the distinctions between determination and volition, faith and free will, self and other, begin to fail us as well.

Fittingly, then, the tradition offers us the richly symbolic anecdotes of Sujata's bowl and the five dreams to suggest the role of grace or providence, the spontaneous, generous radiance of the truth itself. But it also gives us a convincing picture of Siddhartha as a human—rather than divine—being, whose untiring efforts brought him to his present state. This was the man who had the courage to turn away from traditional paradigms whenever his quest for truth led him elsewhere. Surely such perseverance had to lead inevitably to the goal?

Siddhartha began his meditation with a 'limbering-up' practice, in which his training under Alara Kalama stood him in good stead. The first phase of the practice entailed a contemplative and exploratory frame of mind with the happy freedom born of seclusion. The second meditation was characterized by inner confidence, a cessation of thought, a growing quiet concentration, with an attendant state of detachment and well-being. The third meditation was pervaded by immaculate mindfulness, free of emotional oscillation. The fourth and final state consisted of an overriding sense of equanimity, unstained by pain or pleasure, sorrow or joy. Siddhartha describes his mind at this point as 'collected and purified, without blemish, free of defilements, grown soft, workable, fixed and immovable'. The coincidence of apparent opposites is already evident in this description: strong but not rigid, malleable but not gullible, this is the fearlessness of total vulnerability, the alert receptivity of surrender, the freedom of complete relinquishment. Resolute yet pliant, his mind was now poised for the final denouement.

Siddhartha had his first breakthrough in the first phase of the night. In what has come to be known as the first True Knowledge, he recollected the innumerable lives he had lived before the present one. 'I recalled many a former existence I had passed through: one birth, two births, three, four, five, ten, twenty, thirty, forty, fifty, a hundred, a thousand, a hundred thousand births in various world periods: "I was there, such was my name such my family, such my caste, my way of life. I experienced such and such good and bad fortune, and such was my end. Having died, I came to life again there, such was my name . . . and such was my end." In this way I recalled many previous existences with their various characteristic features and circumstances. This knowledge I gained in the first watch of the night.'

In the second watch of the night, he gained a vital insight into the law of ethical causality: 'With the heavenly eye, purified and beyond the range of human vision, I saw how beings vanish and come to be again. I saw high and low, brilliant and insignificant, and how each obtained according to his karma a favourable or painful rebirth. I recognized: "Those beings who make evil use of body, speech and thought will obtain after the breaking-up of the body at death a painful rebirth, they will sink down, perish, and (go to) hell. But those who make good use of body, speech and thought will obtain a favourable rebirth, and (go to) heaven."'

As the approaching dawn silvered the eastern horizon, the final and decisive insight occurred. Siddhartha now had the direct perception of the origin and cessation of suffering, freedom from the inexorable law of endless becoming: 'I directed my mind to the knowledge of the destruction of the influences and knew it as it really is: "This is suffering, this is its cause, this is its cessation, and this is the path that leads to its cessation." And as I recognized this, my mind was free from the influences of sense-desire, of becoming and of ignorance. And the knowledge rose in me: "Rebirth (for me) is destroyed, I have completed the holy life, done what had to be done, there is no more becoming for me!"'

There is a mystic's exultation in the following utterance: 'Seeking but not finding the House Builder,/ I travelled through the round of countless births:/ O painful is birth ever and ever again./ House Builder, you have now been seen;/ You shall not build the house again./ Your rafters have been broken (down);/ Your ridge pole is demolished too./ My mind has now attained the unformed nirvana/ And reached the end of every kind of craving.'

The Buddhist tradition offers an alternative description of the great event. In one account, Siddhartha discovers with a focussed and attentive mind the serial links in the chain of causation that binds humanity to the cycle of birth, suffering and death: 'What is there when ageing and death come to be? What is their necessary condition? Then with ordered attention I came to understand: Birth is there when ageing and death come to be; birth is a necessary condition for them.' With growing clarity he then arrived at an experiential understanding of the mechanism of the karmic wheel: he realized that becoming is a necessary condition for birth; clinging a necessary condition for becoming; craving for clinging; feeling for craving; contact for feeling; the six senses for contact; name and form for the senses; and consciousness for name and form. He discovered that with the cessation of name and form, there would be a cessation of individuated consciousness.

And so, like 'a man wandering in a forest wilderness (who) found an ancient path, an ancient trail, travelled by men of old', Siddhartha too stumbled upon 'an ancient city, an ancient royal capital' by following the trail travelled by the 'Fully Enlightened Ones of Old'. With a mystic's heightened vision of the source of human delusion, he was now able, in an inspired and incisive formulation, to diagnose the disease that assailed the world. He perceived the cause, the possibility of its removal, and was able to prescribe the cure.

In a third description of the life-transformational insight, the tradition tells how Siddhartha discerned the naked, luminous truth beyond the world of conditioned acts and ideas. 'In case of material form, of feeling (of pleasure, pain or neither), of perception, of formations, of consciousness, what is the gratification, what the danger, what the escape? Then I thought: In the case of each, the bodily pleasure and mental joy that arise in dependence on these things are the gratification; the fact that these things are all impermanent, painful and subject to change, is the danger; the disciplining and abandoning of desire and lust for them is the escape.'

Although each of the accounts offers us an intellectual trajectory of Siddhartha's thought process during the enlightenment, they do not attempt to offer a glimpse of the experience itself. The Buddha himself famously made no attempt to do so. As a state that transcends every dualistic category, nirvana, or the direct unmediated knowledge of the truth, defies all description for it lies beyond the binaries in which all human language is rooted.

However, it is possible to make certain observations about Siddhartha's seminal insight. For one, contrary to popular perception, it did not occur in a single blinding flash. It seems to have been a process of growing lucidity, of deepening understanding, which lasted an entire night. For another, it emphatically did not entail a trance state, an out-of-body experience or cosmic revelation. The most distinctive feature of Siddhartha's nirvana is the fact that it involved mind and gut, intellect and intuition, rationality and insight—in modern parlance, the left and the right brain. It seems to have been a period of heightened clarity, intense alertness, and a vibrant dynamic sense of presence. The repeated phrase, 'ordered attention', and his reiteration that he 'directed' his mind to various troubling questions, suggests that this was a man with an inspired awareness of all his faculties. This was certainly not a state of blissful self-forgetfulness, 'God-intoxication' or divine possession.

His later teaching indicates that a significant and profound insight at the time was his perception of the individual as a shifting aggregate of habits, memories and desires rather than an objective 'thing', a fluid karmic construct rather than an unchanging entity with an immovable centre. He also saw the entire cosmos as a journey rather than a destination, a web of interconnected strands, a ceaseless stream of interrelated energy patterns, changing images and appearances. Significantly, what he perceived was a process, with neither producer nor product. This insight—which points so temptingly today to an Einsteinian view of the universe, rather than a Newtonian one—seems to have cut through layers of conditioning like a knife through butter, and freed Siddhartha entirely from the clinging and grasping reflexes of the mind. This was the good news that he was later to take to the world from Bodhgaya: the inherent transience, interdependence and no-thingness of the phenomenal world, which reveals the pointlessness of all ego-driven human activity.

And what happens when the ego-self recognizes its own fictional identity? What lies beyond the play of phantoms, beyond the giant wheel of cause–effect, past–future, memory–desire? What emerges when the frozen cluster of habits and propensities that makes up the individual being begins to thaw? What happens when the lights come on and the show stops, when we refuse to suspend our disbelief any longer? What happens when we stop colluding in our own delusion? Tantalizingly, the Buddha left that unanswered. Not surprisingly, some have interpreted this to mean that the ultimate reality is the annihilation of the self. Others have interpreted it as the absorption of the self into the infinite.

But the Buddha was canny enough to realize that to offer an answer would have been to perpetuate an even fiercer storm of dialectic, a maelstrom of echoes, of interpretation and counter-interpretation. His wise legacy, therefore, is a heritage of silence. Of unassailable incontrovertible silence. It is a silence that lays to rest in one swift stroke the bristling, arrogant metaphysician in each one of us—and awakens the latent mystic.

The Last Temptation

Revelling in the triumphant peace attendant on this clarified vision, the Awakened One spent the next seven weeks in seclusion. One can imagine the mystic silently celebrating his awakening after long years of struggle. The scriptures tell us that Mara, the Tempter, the Demon of Delusion, who had been plaguing the young seeker at various junctures in the past, now renewed his attacks. A recurrent (almost Mephistophelean) presence in the Buddhist scriptures, Mara has been variously viewed as a literary device, a nature myth, even as a personification of the inner workings of the Buddha's mind.

This trial marks Mara's desperate attempt to shatter the Buddha's new-won equanimity. He cast stones at the untiring meditator, but these, fittingly, turned to flowers. He then sent his three beautiful daughters, Arati, Trishna and Rati to distract the Buddha, but these blandishments proved futile as well. He proceeded to unleash tempest, fire and flood, the three causes of world-destruction, followed by the thick impenetrable blackness of the void (tapping the deepest human fear of complete dissolution). However, each of these attacks was repelled. Muchalinda, the Serpent King, is said to have protected the young contemplative under his hood, and the Buddha's meditation continued unruffled.

Perhaps this is how the Buddha would have remained until the end of his days—the anonymous mystic, who lived and died in the wilds of Uruvela, unrecorded, unsung like so many others. However, Tapussa and Bhallika, two merchants, who met him at this point (and later became his first lay followers), probably urged him to instruct them. This may have kindled in him the impulse to impart his wisdom, but also made him aware of just how difficult that task would be. He now realized that the truth he had stumbled upon was profound and elusive, requiring more than sterile logic, and yet, demanding more than blind faith. The temptation to lead a life of solitude was perhaps the subtlest challenge that Mara cast in the Buddha's way.

The Pali texts record his inner dilemma in terms of a conversation with the god Brahma Sahampati. 'This world delights in the pleasures of the senses,' reasoned the Buddha, 'but my teaching aims at the renunciation of all attachments and the destruction of craving. If I were to teach this doctrine, which goes against the stream and people did not understand me, that would cause me much weariness and trouble.' And so he favoured the life of a recluse. But luckily for the world, Brahma Sahampati was persuasive. He pleaded with him to teach the truth for the sake of those 'with little dust over their eyes'. 'If they do not hear the Dharma,' entreated the god, 'they will be lost.'

And so the awakening at Bodhgaya did not remain a private discovery. The Buddha acknowledged that it could spell a profound transformation for those in the right state of receptivity. As for the rest of humanity, once the truth of the insight ignited the bushel of karmic chaff, the conflagration was a certainty.

It was—and still remains, or so it is held by those inspired by the path of Shakyamuni—only a matter of time.

Tathagata, the Master

'*Him I call a Brahmin who clings not to pleasure, no more than water to a lotus leaf or mustard seed to the tip of a needle.*' (Chapter 26, Dhammapada)

So the Buddha emerged from the forest of Uruvela to share the fiercely radical insight that the 'ancient trail' he had discovered belonged not merely to a coterie of spiritual savants. It belonged to all who wanted to become the navigators of their own destinies. He returned not to repudiate tradition, but to remind people that the only tradition worth cherishing is the one that does not discriminate among its inheritors. 'You say this in faith,' he later told Ananda, his faithful disciple. 'I know it from experience.' The Buddha spent the rest of his life reiterating that the experience could be ours.

The result of this decision to return to the world was a ministry that was to last more than forty years. Shakyamuni's teaching blew like a breath of fresh air through the towns and forests of the Gangetic plain, vitalizing the lives of a cross-section of society: punditry and peasantry, nobles and merchants, thieves and courtesans, sceptics and intellectuals. The doctrine that he proclaimed was not a belief-system to which he sought to convert others as much as a clear-sighted diagnosis, an axiomatic truth that he sought to help them recognize. His unique mix of charisma and kindliness, his radiant presence, his urbane and courteous manner in debate, and the bracing vitality of his teaching won him a ready listenership, and a burgeoning tribe of adherents to a way that knew no partisanship.

The first two individuals with whom he wanted to share his insight were his former teachers, Alara Kalama and Udraka Ramaputra, both evolved practitioners with 'little dust over their eyes'. However, with his prescient inner gaze he divined that both had died recently. He then decided to seek out the five disciples who had attended to him during the ascetic phase of his struggle. Discerning their whereabouts, he set out for the Deer Park in Rishipatana (modern-day Sarnath) near Varanasi.

The initial reaction of the five was withering disbelief. This was, after all, the teacher who had fallen from grace when he abandoned the challenges of a life of asceticism. However, there was something about the serenity of his countenance and the poise of his bearing that impressed them in spite of themselves. They realized, perhaps subconsciously, that they were in the presence of an Awakened One, a Tathagata ('One Who Has Come And Gone This Way' or a 'Thus-goer'), and they gradually 'opened their hearts to knowledge'.

The historic first sermon on the night of the full moon of July was the Dharma Chakra Pravartana Sutra—the Teaching that Set in Motion the Wheel of Righteousness—in which the Buddha articulated his doctrine for the first time. His human audience numbered only five, but legend has it that the gods listened close, and even the nearby deer found themselves irresistibly attracted to this trailblazing wisdom delivered with an air of quiet authority. The seasoned explorer of the inner path spoke of the two extremes of sensuality and mortification, and then unfolded the practical roadmap of the Middle Way upon which he had stumbled. He addressed the central core of the human condition as he spoke of Suffering, the Origin of Suffering, the Cessation of Suffering, and the Way leading to the Cessation of Suffering: the Noble Eightfold Path. As long as this was mere cognitive understanding, said the Tathagata, 'I did not claim to be enlightened.' But now 'my heart's deliverance is unassailable; this is the last birth; there is no more renewal of being'.

The first to understand the teaching was Kaundinya, the senior ascetic, who was admitted into the Holy Life with the words: 'Come, bhikshu. The Law is well proclaimed. Live the Holy Life for the complete ending of suffering.' As the Buddha continued to instruct the group on the impermanence of material form and consciousness, the spotless vision of the Dharma, the inexorable natural law, rose in the minds of the other bhikshus as well. They were also included within the fold by the Buddha in a historic gesture that marked the beginning of the sangha, the community of monks. There were now, the canon tells us, six arhants—fully realized beings—in the world.

The seventh to attain enlightenment was Yasha, a rich merchant of Varanasi, who awoke one morning and had a sudden visceral experience of the emptiness of sensory pleasure. He saw his attendants in various stages of slumber—one with her hair unfastened, one dribbling, the other muttering—and was seized with revulsion at the other side of the world of pleasure, the dross, the rancidity, the stale morning-after miasma that follows a night of indulgence. He rose and left his abode forever. Deliverance awaited him at the Deer Park, and he soon joined the ranks of the realized. His parents and wife became the first lay adherents of the Path, and several friends and acquaintances from leading merchant families in Varanasi followed suit.

When the Buddha's following had swelled to sixty-one, he urged his monks to disperse and disseminate the doctrine among the people: 'Go not any two together. Proclaim, O Bhikshus, the Dharma that is good in the beginning, good in the middle, good in the end. There will be some,' he added, not without a touch of wryness, 'who will understand.' He later authorized the monks to ordain their converts with a formulation that is repeated by adherents all over the world to this very day: 'I take my refuge in the Buddha. I take my refuge in the Dharma. I take my refuge in the Sangha.'

The biographies proceed to offer a triumphal chronicle of the conversions accomplished by the Buddha and his monks as they wandered across the terrain of north-eastern India: from the fire-worshippers and their thousand followers to Shariputra and Maudgalyayana (whom the Buddha accurately prophesied would be his 'chief disciples') and their two hundred and fifty followers; from King Bimbisara of Magadha to King Pasenadi of Kosala; from Angulimala, the thief, to Amrapali, the lovely courtesan. While the numbers could well have been inflated and the success rate exaggerated by canonical propagandists, the varied composition of the Buddha's following does testify to the way his inspired doctrine was embraced across a spectrum of backgrounds. The Buddha seemed inclined to define his role as physician rather than proselytizer, as compassionate cartographer rather than saviour. What he adopted was not a mere populist strategy, for his teachings promised no quick-fix solution to life's problems. But it remained truly democratic, for it held out the promise of self-realization for all.

A glimpse of this vigorous and transformational teaching by a master at the height of his powers can still be found in the famous Fire Sermon, delivered to the newly converted fire-worshipping ascetics at Gayashirsha. From its opening line—'Bhikshus, all is burning'—the sutra arrests our attention with its vividly dystopic, deeply unsettling view of the phenomenal world. 'All things,' said the Tathagata, 'are on fire; the eye is on fire; forms are on fire; eye-consciousness is on fire; the impressions received by the eye are on fire; and whatever sensation originates in the impressions received by the eye is likewise on fire. And with what are these things on fire? With the fires of lust, anger and illusion, with these are they on fire, and so with the other senses, and so with the mind. Wherefore the wise man conceives disgust for these things of the senses, and being divested of desire for the things of the senses, he removes from his heart the cause of suffering.'

While some were struck by the perceptive, exultantly egalitarian nature of the teachings, others were mesmerized by the Buddha's presence, his unwavering equipoise, the sense he exuded of a man at deep peace with himself. Not surprisingly, wealthy householders of both sexes, such as Anathapindika and Vishakha of Shravasti, as well as kings, like Bimbisara, became staunch patrons, donating lavishly to the Order in terms of land, retreats for the rains, medical amenities, clothes and food, to show their gratitude to the benevolent donor of the Dharma. There is a jubilant air in King Bimbisara's declaration that all his five childhood aspirations had now been fulfilled: to ascend the throne, to encounter a fully enlightened man, to honour him, to be instructed by him, and to have understood the instruction.

The Buddha's return to his family abode in Kapilavastu at the earnest entreaty of his father in 527 BCE is an interesting anecdote in the canon. Seven years earlier, Siddhartha's parting message to his charioteer was to inform his family of his unshakeable resolve: '(Tell them) either he will extinguish old age and death, and then you shall quickly see him again; or he will go to perdition, because his strength has failed him and he could not achieve his purpose.' The determined young pilgrim of Kapilavastu had now returned with his mission accomplished: a victorious seer. It was a dramatic moment when the yellow-robed monk enunciated his doctrine of deathlessness before the very kinsfolk who had given him life. His father, Shuddhodana, attained an advanced stage of realization on hearing the teachings. Four years later, the ruler was to die a full-fledged arhant.

Perhaps the most poignant moment of the visit—also an index of how far the Buddha had journeyed from his past life as householder—was when Yashodhara sent her young son, Rahula, to his father with the words: 'That is your father, Rahula. Go ask him for your inheritance.' There is pathos in these lines. If one listens closer, one can also perhaps hear fury, impotence, seething irony. The words draw attention to Yashodhara's life in the past seven years, condemned to premature widowhood, a single mother trapped in her husband's home without the consolations of a lover and companion. Did she nurse a flickering hope that the Buddha would be shamed into some awareness of his neglected parental obligation?

If she did, she was to be disappointed for the man before her was no longer the Siddhartha she had once known; this was the Sage of the Shakyas, whose compassion now extended beyond narrow familial frontiers to embrace all of humanity. Rahula was not exempt either. The Buddha looked upon him with a gaze of aloof benignity, and blessed him in the most gracious way he knew. He asked Shariputra to ordain him into the monastic life. Not surprisingly, this evoked a storm of consternation. Shuddhodana finally implored his son not to admit children into his order without parental consent. The Buddha acquiesced, but in the case of Rahula, it was already too late. He had already joined the fold, his ordination having been sanctioned by none other than his own father.

There must have been several who were dazzled by the Buddha's charismatic presence, and hastily took monastic vows without quite being aware of its implications. Nanda, the Buddha's half-brother, was one of these. There is a touch of levity in the canonical account of how he was given to wearing ironed robes, anointing his eyes, and using a glazed alms bowl—signs of a vestigial attachment to the life of comfort and ease he had left behind. Eventually, the Buddha intervened and drily reminded him that such behaviour did not befit an alms-gatherer. Gradually, the conceited Nanda mended his ways and was later to become a forest-dweller who wore only rags.

The predicament of Rahula, as a 'celebrity-offspring' as it were, was not without its problems either. One day, several years after his admission, while following his father on his alms round, the eighteen-year-old's thoughts began to wander. He idly speculated what his life might have been had his father become the universal monarch as had been predicted of him if he had chosen another path. The Buddha discerned these thoughts. Ever the uncompromising teacher, he was quick to deflate his son's fanciful notions. He proceeded to deliver a stern lecture on the mutability of the phenomenal world. 'Rahula, any kind of material form, whether past, future or present, in oneself or external, coarse or fine, inferior or superior, far or near, should be regarded as it actually is with right understanding: This is not mine, this is not what I am, this is not myself.' Feelings, perceptions, mental formations and even consciousness, he added, should be regarded in the same way.

Chastened by this public rebuke, Rahula lagged behind and spent the rest of the day in meditation. In the evening, he asked his father for instruction on the mindfulness of breathing. Two years later, after receiving the Full Admission, he became an arhant on hearing the Buddha's discourse on impermanence. The frequently reiterated formulation that 'all that is subject to arising is subject to cessation' penetrated residual layers of conditioning and suddenly became an experiential reality. And Rahula finally came into his full inheritance as his father's son.

An important development in the history of the Order occurred soon after the Buddha paid his second visit to Kapilavastu on the death of his father, probably in 523 BCE. His widowed foster mother, Mahaprajapati Gautami, accompanied by a group of women, followed him all the way to Vaishali. Exhausted, dusty, swollen-footed, but with her sense of mission intact, the tenacious matriarch, who had shorn her hair and donned the yellow robes of renunciation, sought her son's permission for women to be inducted into the homeless life. The Enlightened One, probably wary of the social implications of such a move in a feudal context, denied her request three times. However, his cousin and senior monk, Ananda, pleaded on her behalf. He eventually won the day by posing an important question: Are women not capable, then, of self-realization? The Tathagata's credo of spiritual equality compelled him to concede that they were. He probably smiled at Ananda's ruse, and capitulated.

Mahaprajapati Gautami and the group of women

were now admitted into a new order of nuns. Some accounts hold that Yashodhara also joined the order at this time. The Master is supposed to have declared ruefully, however, that the growth of the Holy Life would be retarded by the admission of women and would last no more than five hundred years. His political acumen and powers of prescience notwithstanding, it is heartening to see that the Buddha was wrong on this score, there being no gender-based impediment to the acceptance of his doctrine in the world.

An interesting proposal for gender equality was later mooted by Mahaprajapati—the first Buddhist nun—when she asked Ananda to request the Buddha to allow monks and nuns to pay homage to their seniors, irrespective of gender. She was obviously uncomfortable with the rule that required even a senior nun to stand up and salute a monk, regardless of whether he was a veteran or a novice. The Buddha was, however, unwilling to accede to her request. Perhaps it is unfair to expect him to challenge and defy every social more of his day. It is also, perhaps, inevitable that he would continue in some respects to be a product of his times. Nonetheless, this is one of those moments in the story when one wishes his radicalism had extended just that bit further.

As the Buddha's community grew, a set of norms and a code of conduct were gradually established, most

of which were based on purely pragmatic considerations.
The practice of the 'rains retreat' for the wandering
monks was a practice instituted by the Buddha himself
a few years after the Order was founded. The *Vinaya
Pitaka* offers a long account leading to the constitution
of a code of rules. When Sudhindra, a rich merchant's
son from a village near Vaishali, returned to have sex
with his wife after having embraced the monastic life,
the Buddha rebuked him roundly for violating a law
based on dispassion. It was at this time that the code of
training rules for monks was apparently constituted, the
first being a ban on sexual intercourse.

The Buddha himself was not in favour of too many
rigid monastic regulations, insisting even on his deathbed
that these remain flexible. When his cousin, Devadatta,
demanded a more ascetic regimen for the monks—forest-
living and a strictly vegetarian diet—the Buddha
emphatically rejected the proposal. He insisted the
monks be free to choose to live either in forests or
villages, and to partake of meat or fish as long as the
animal had not been killed for their benefit. Even the
monks' sartorial code of a triple robe was instituted after
balancing the principle of austerity against the equally
imperative need of protection against the cold.

The institutionalization of the faith in his own
lifetime brought its share of inner tensions, and meant
that the reclusive mystic also had to play the roles of

administrator and arbitrator. Several instances indicate
that the Buddha regarded these rules only as a means to
an end, and was concerned that they should be
interpreted in terms of the spirit rather than the letter.
Nine years after the Order was established, an internal
quarrel broke out among the monks at Kosambi over a
trifling incident of community etiquette. This soon
escalated into a feud and a schism seemed imminent.
The community was divided over the issue: some
believed the offending monk should be excommunicated,
while others held that he was innocent since he had done
nothing intentionally malevolent. Initially, the Buddha
did his best to restore harmony among the litigious
monks, but soon a hermit's distaste at the pettiness of
human ego battles came to the fore. He withdrew into
seclusion, choosing to 'walk like a tusker in the woods
alone'. Only after the wrangling monks had settled their
affairs and reinstated the monk (who, in turn, begged
pardon), was the Buddha appeased.

Once at Shravasti, the venerable monk
Mahakashyapa is said to have asked the Buddha why
there now seemed to be more rules and fewer liberated
monks. The Buddha replied: 'When creatures are
degenerating and the Good Law is disappearing, there
come to be more training rules and few bhikshus become
established in the final knowledge.' He added, however,
that all was not bleak—there were still several respectful

monks, and the Dharma would not disappear all at once.

In yet another instance that throws light on the Buddha's attitude to rules, a monk complained that he found it difficult to train in the 150-odd rules of conduct that came up for recitation every fortnight. The Master suggested that he train only in three: the rule of higher virtue, higher consciousness and higher understanding. These, said the Buddha, were sufficient for enlightenment, and the monk, we are told, was soon free of lust, hate and delusion.

The Buddha asserted time and again, however, that far more important than a doctrinaire observance of piety was an essentially humane approach towards all living beings. In his later years, the Buddha and Ananda, his conscientious attendant, found a monk, afflicted with dysentery, lying alone in his lodging, in a pool of urine and excrement. The ageing Buddha and Ananda personally cleaned him and helped him up on his bed. Immediately after this, the Master summoned an assembly of the bhikshus and reminded them of the urgent need of community care: 'Brethren, you have no mother and father to take care of you. If you will not take care of each other, who else, I ask, will do so? Brethren, he who would wait on me, let him wait on the sick.' It is a moment when the Shakyan Sage's voice seems to anticipate that of the mystic of Galilee.

One of the most arresting incidents in the course of

the Great Master's ministry is the tale of his encounter with Angulimala. The latter was a hardened criminal, whose peculiar and somewhat grisly idiosyncrasy was to kill harmless wayfarers, cut off their fingers and string them together in a necklace of digits he wore around his neck. The Tathagata was cautioned by the shepherds, peasants and fellow-travellers against taking the road that was Angulimala's beat. He paid no attention to the warning.

When Angulimala caught sight of this unknown mendicant walking unhurriedly down his road, he was taken aback by his effrontery. He raced after him, but could not catch up, although the Buddha maintained a steady walking pace. Finally, a breathless Angulimala called out to him to stop. The Buddha's reply is justifiably famous: 'I have stopped, Angulimala; it is time you stopped as well.' The bandit was puzzled by the reply. The Buddha explained that while he had forsworn violence against every living creature, Angulimala still lacked the necessary inner restraint—he had, therefore, 'not stopped'. This simple reply marked the conversion of a confirmed sociopath. He flung down his weapons, begged forgiveness and asked to be admitted into the Sangha. The Buddha welcomed him with his two simple trademark words: 'Come, bhikshu'. When King Pasenadi learnt of this conversion, he is said to have marvelled at the Great Sage's ability to 'subdue the unsubdued, quiet the unquieted' without punishment.

While the progress of the doctrine was rapid, the Buddha's ministry was not free from scandal. There was a time, we are told, when the members of other sects did their bit to discredit the sangha by alleging promiscuity and even murder, the issue being the death of a nun named Sundari. The Master instructed his indignant monks to remain unruffled by the rumours, and assured them that they would die a natural death in a week, which, as is the habit with rumours, they did.

The mendicant's life was not without hardship either. Alms-gathering meant living with daily uncertainty, but also negotiating the knee-jerk cynicism of the laity towards self-professed men of god. Eleven years after his enlightenment, the Tathagata encountered a Brahmin who poured on him the scorn typical of the economically self-reliant for the dependent: 'I plough and sow, and having finished work, I eat. You too, shramana, should plough and sow, and then you would have food.' The Teacher was unimpressed with this self-righteous argument, however, and was ready with a rejoinder: 'I sow faith, my plough is wisdom, energy is my draught-ox, the fruit of my labour is Deathlessness. Whoever performs such work is freed from all sorrow.' The Brahmin was abashed and sought to make amends. The Buddha accepted his apology, but with quiet dignity, refused his offer of milk and rice.

The Buddha's abhorrence of animal sacrifice, a rampant practice in his time, has been well documented. While such ritual killing outraged his legendary sense of compassion for all living beings, it also offended his spirit of rationality and he was at pains to point out that a vicarious atonement of one's deeds was a karmic impossibility. We are told that he was successful in convincing Kutadanta (a prosperous Brahmin who planned a sacrifice of seven hundred bulls, oxen, cows, goats and rams) that meditation and adherence to an ethical life were the only sacrifices that had any validity. At the same time, he was pragmatic enough to realize that universal vegetarianism was a utopian ideal. He permitted his monks, as alms-gatherers, to accept meat, but instructed them to refuse it if they had seen, heard or suspected that the animal had been specially slaughtered for their benefit.

When the Buddha was seventy-two years old, his first cousin and senior monk, Devadatta, consumed by ambition, attempted to usurp his place. The legend of the boyhood squabble over the ownership of the wounded bird provides a psychological rationale for this event. This is described in detail in the *Vinaya Pitaka*: Devadatta's devious machinations to win the favour of Prince Ajatashatru, his brazen act of asking the Buddha permission to rule the sangha on the grounds that the latter was old and unfit; and the Buddha's scathing refusal and public denunciation of his cousin.

The Pitaka proceeds to relate how the spurned Devadatta instigated Ajatashatru to commit parricide, and further conspired with him to hire assassins to kill the Buddha. When the latter failed, the desperate Devadatta attempted the terrible deed himself. He hurled a rock at the Buddha, and even let a wild elephant loose on him. It was to no avail, however. The Buddha foiled each of these plots. Particularly attractive is the tale of the Buddha simply engulfing Nalagiri, the mad elephant, with his immense compassion, so that 'the confrontation between the two tuskers' turned into a display of mutual affection and respect.

Devadatta's final ploy was to create a schism in the community by urging a more rigorously ascetic life for the monks. Predictably, the Master rejected the proposal, and Devadatta with his splinter group of five hundred monks set up a separate base for themselves at Gayashirsha. However, senior monks Shariputra and Maudgalyayana soon won the secessionists back again with a rousing joint sermon. When Devadatta realized that he had been abandoned, he was so incensed that hot blood supposedly gushed from his mouth.

The canon does not relate the actual circumstances of Devadatta's death, but according to legend, the earth opened, swallowed him up and consigned him to hell. While one can safely assume that much of this account is fictional, there is probably some truth in the account that he nursed ambitions of superseding the Buddha, and challenged his authority on more than one occasion. The Master later told his disciples that Devadatta's folly lay in three factors: overweening ambition, wrong company, and most importantly, his contentment with the attainment of supernormal powers over the goal of self-realization.

Without Tarrying, Without Hurrying

The life of the Buddha, unlike that of many great saints, is not a catalogue of flamboyant miracles. Would miracles have won him more converts? Perhaps. But for the wrong reasons, and the Buddha reveals a strong distaste for the use of manipulative means to swell his constituency. He refused to use psychic gifts or paranormal powers to heal the sick, raise the dead or uplift the weak. This, he held, could only foster a jingoistic faith, a blind self-abnegation rather than a spiritual conviction of any depth or discernment. At the Pavarika Grove in Nalanda, a householder's son, Kevadha, suggested that the Tathagata appoint a monk to work a miracle so that Nalanda's faith in the Dharma might increase. The Sage replied that though he did possess certain supernormal powers, he was no more than a magician if he used them merely to impress people.

More importantly, they offered no enduring escape from the central human problem: suffering. The only power he was prepared to use was the 'marvel of guidance'—spiritual instruction—since this served the higher objective of leading seekers to the other shore.

Once in Kosambi, the Master picked up a handful of leaves and asked the monks what was more plentiful—the leaves in his hand or those on the trees. Those in the forest, replied the monks. So also, said the Buddha, the things that I have known by direct knowledge are far more than what I have taught. Why did he withhold some aspects of knowledge? The familiar answer: 'Because they bring no benefit, they do not lead to the cessation of suffering, to nirvana.'

The Buddha's mistrust of miracle-mongering extended to an impatience with superstition and hollow convention as well. A humorous account relates how when the Teacher sneezed in the middle of a sermon, the monks chorused the conventional response: 'Long life to you, Lord.' The rational Master, vexed at the interruption, forbade the custom on the grounds that it was a mere tokenism. Later, however, when disapproving householders complained that the alms-gathering monks did not make the polite observance, the Buddha revoked his decision and permitted them to continue the practice.

Many of the Tathagata's listeners found their entire

world view transformed in a single stroke by a deceptively simple insight, a spontaneous parable, or a seemingly minor clarification of doctrine. As did the wanderer Dighanakha, who informed the Buddha that he espoused a theory of non-attachment, having 'no liking for anything'. The Buddha listened patiently, then gently drew his attention to the subtle egotism of this stance—for even attachment to this intellectual position was a type of grasping, born of a need to retain some marker of identity. 'The Dispassionate One disputes with none and sides with none,' declared the Master. On hearing this, Shariputra, his prime disciple, attained enlightenment and Dighanakha was inspired to join the fold.

Fundamental to the Tathagata's teaching was the maintenance of a creative tension between the extremes of self-mortification and self-indulgence. As the Buddha had anticipated, this delicate balance was not always an easy one to maintain, particularly for the new aspirant. Once when the Master happened to be staying in Vaishali, he delivered a stirring talk to his monks on the contemplation of the impermanence of the body—its frailty and the inevitability of its decay. When he returned from a retreat two weeks later, he discovered that several monks had been consumed by physical revulsion and had been driven to suicide. On hearing this, the Buddha immediately called a meeting, and disabused the assembly of the notion of the inherent evil of the flesh. He then instructed them on the mindfulness of breathing, as an alternative purificatory practice—a means of 'making evil objects vanish like a summer shower banishes dust and dirt'.

Sona, a monk, found himself in the archetypal seeker's quandary: despite his ardent spiritual practice, he was plagued by thoughts about the material world. The Master divined his thoughts, and instead of a dry homily, offered him an evocative metaphor to suggest a new approach to his spiritual commitment. He reminded him of the veena (an instrument that Sona had played as a layman) which cannot be played when the strings are either too taut or too slack, but only when evenly tuned. So also, said the Tathagata, in what is now a justifiably legendary insight, 'over-striving leads to agitation and under-striving to slackness'.

On yet another occasion, when asked how he had managed to cross the flood of suffering, the Tathagata's reply endorsed yet again the Middle Way between the extremes of indulgence and fanaticism: 'Without tarrying and without hurrying, I crossed the flood. When I tarried, I sank; when I hurried, I was whirled around. Only when I neither tarried nor hurried did I cross the flood.'

Despite his emphasis on the individual determining his own salvation, the Buddha's ideal of the sangha was a template of interdependence and community responsibility, and involved a vital connection between clergy and laity. Moreover, spiritual development, in the Master's view, was of no use if it was a mere evasion of social responsibility or simply a product of psychological immaturity. The Buddha pointed out to Thera, a monk who preferred a reclusive life, the importance of living in community until the ideal of 'living alone' was genuinely understood and fully internalized. True solitude, said the Awakened One, is not merely shunning company, not mere misanthropy. It is that state when 'what is past is left behind, what is future is renounced, and lust and the desire for selfhood acquired in the present is quite put away'.

Moderation was always the key for a teacher who enjoined a path between sterile rationality and naive faith. When the Kalamas, the people of Keshaputra in the Kosala region, asked the Master for advice on how to distinguish between the genuine and spurious spiritual teacher, the Buddha was quick to appreciate their honesty and courage in expressing their doubts. The incident is a reminder that mistrust about the godman-and-guru phenomenon is by no means merely a modern-day preoccupation. Offering them a strategy of self-determination, the Buddha urged them not to rely on hearsay, tradition, legend, scripture or conjecture. He suggested that they evaluate each case themselves on the basis of whether they felt the monk was free of lust, hate, delusion, covetousness and ill-will, and exuded an air of compassion, equanimity and unwavering mindfulness.

The same refusal to perpetuate oppressive hierarchies through excessive centralization is evident in his firm refusal to the two Brahmin monks who sought permission to translate his doctrine into Sanskrit metre. The Master insisted that classicizing his doctrine would do more harm than good, and issued strict instructions that his word was meant to be learnt only in one's own language.

The Buddha seems to have dealt with sceptics in the course of his life with equanimity. In the course of a philosophical dispute in Vaishali, a monk named Sachaka asked him whether he had ever slept in the daytime. He obviously considered this a human failing that enlightened beings ought to have vanquished! The Tathagata replied that in the last month of the summer, he had on occasion fallen asleep after the alms round, 'mindful and fully aware'. The monk countered that this could be construed as a sign of delusion. The imperturbable Master replied that only he who had not abandoned the acquisitive impulses of the ego could be deemed deluded. Although the monk remained unconvinced by this logic, he could not help observing that the Master Gautama remained unruffled and his countenance unflushed even at the most provocative questions.

While the Buddha was quick to offer help to the doubter, he was astute enough to distinguish between genuine spiritual uncertainty and the nit-picking impulse of the intellectual merely out to flex some metaphysical bicep. 'What happens to the Perfect One after death?', 'Does the self exist?', 'Is the world eternal or temporary, finite or infinite?' Time and again he responded to these questions with silence or with the firm reply: 'What I describe is suffering and the cessation of suffering.' All the other questions, he maintained, were superfluous and only ensnared one further in the thicket of opinion. If he agreed with the wanderer Vachhagota on whether the self exists, he could potentially foster a theory of eternalism. If he disagreed with him, he could endorse a view of annihilationism. Silence, he maintained, was a preferable strategy.

How then did he see his pedagogic role, this teacher who refused to perform miracles, who kept an obstinate silence in the face of persistent metaphysical questions, who countered opposition with benign detachment? The following incident provides a clue.

Why, asked one Brahmin, do only some disciples attain enlightenment, despite the fact that all have the Tathagata as a guide? The Buddha replied characteristically with an analogy. Suppose the Brahmin were to give two people the directions to Rajagriha, why did only one reach and the other take a wrong turn and get lost? 'What have I to do with that, Master Gautama?' protested the Brahmin. 'I am simply the one who shows the way.'

So too, said the Great Shramana, am I.

Dharma, the Eternal Law

'Our life is shaped by our mind; we become what we think.' (Chapter 1, Dhammapada)

What would you do if your house were on fire? Conduct an investigation into the causes of the devastation? Sit down to pray that your life and possessions be saved? Make a list of all that you are about to lose? Analyse the chemical composition of fire? Ponder the state of your future life? Draw up an architectural blueprint for a new home? The questions are, of course, rhetorical. The answer, obviously: none of the above.

The burning house is one of the most evocative metaphors employed by the Buddha to impress upon his listeners the urgency of the need for liberation. It also reveals the ultimate futility of all metaphysical speculation. The nature of the first cause, the essence of the transmigrating self, the existence of the noumenon—all these questions are consigned to the realm of cerebral gymnastics, navel-gazing, idle procrastination. The only meaningful option in an existential crisis is to take immediate and decisive action. The burning house is the metaphor of a pragmatist, not a pundit; of a spiritual activist, not a theologian.

And yet, the Buddha would not have you believe that he is the heroic fireman, the douser of flames. He does not promise to rescue you. He trusts you to be able to do it yourself. His role is to show you how. Although the obvious solution is to leave the burning house, the Buddha's message is clearly not one of facile escapism. What he proceeds to offer is not the dogma of defeatism, but a licence to self-determination. Leave the site of the catastrophe, he suggests, but not in a state of uncontrolled panic. Remember that the fire can be mastered, but first it must be acknowledged.

And so perhaps it is time to pause in the narrative and examine the nature of the Buddha's spiritual bequest. What exactly did he offer his listeners other than the radiance of his presence? Centuries later, when the personal charisma of the man has long faded, when there are newer faces and more accessible voices, when strategies of spiritual propaganda have become far more aggressively foot-in-the-door, why do so many still find themselves returning to some of his basic insights?

Primarily because the dharma he offers does not necessitate a belief in an old god or a new. It does not involve sacrament, scripture or saviour. Its only demand is that the seeker be a strenuous self-reliant practitioner, committed to a life of ethical diligence, unflinching psychological self-examination and meditation. It is an invitation not to passivity, but praxis. 'We wage war, Brethren; therefore are we called warriors . . . For lofty virtue, for high endeavour, for sublime wisdom—for these things do we wage war.'

Was the path to which the Buddha invited his following particularly different from the 'ancient trail' of the Upanishads? Certainly, he did not regard himself as an inventor of a new faith, but as a revealer of a natural law. Like the Upanishads, he challenged Vedic authority, accepted the law of karma, rejected ritualism and affirmed the importance of experiential self-knowledge. However, the old trail to which he invited people was now redefined and cleansed of inconsistency and compromise. It was a way that refused to discriminate between the chosen and the disinherited. This 'Protestant' spirit and his inspired restatement of certain doctrines marked an important rupture with the past, which is why he also termed it new, 'never heard before'.

What does one need to believe in, in order to be a Buddhist? While there is a fundamental doctrine (based on his formulations of the nature of existence as he experienced it), the Buddha's is essentially the path of de-conditioning, rather than fresh indoctrination. He simply urges people to clear their eyes of myriad distorted perspectives—bedazzled as they are by samsara's hall of mirrors—and see things by the common light of day. What he offers is not so much a new creed as a description of the way things really are (yathabhuta-jnanadarshana).

This tormenting yet fascinating world we live in, he tells us, has three basic characteristics. The first feature—

which comprises the core of Buddhist wisdom—is impermanence or anitya. Everything in the world—all conditioned reality—has a beginning and an end. A single organism undergoes a variety of overt and covert psychological, physical and molecular changes from moment to moment. Whether it is a butterfly that lives for a day, a human being who lives eighty years, or a Brahma who lives millions of years, all are transient. Even the gods are not exempt from a geriatric fate and death! And yet, humans choose wilfully to shut out this unsettling truth, and cleave desperately to the comforting delusion of fixity, in terms of attachment to the material world, a system of beliefs or an immutable self.

The second feature the Buddha asks us to acknowledge is the ubiquity of suffering. This is the subject of the First Noble Truth he preached at the Deer Park in Rishipatana. He probably chose it over the theme of impermanence, in order to make an immediate appeal to his listeners' experience of the world. Certainly, few mystics have spoken about suffering with the same degree of eloquence and empathy. The Buddha's notion of dukkha, if you think about it, is broad enough to encompass every conceivable kind of affliction and discontent: the million unrecorded private torments, the despair born of centuries of social and political servitude, the raging inner conflicts, the paradoxical fears of failure and success, of death and of life, the existential unease, the Weltschmerz, the 'out-of-kilterness', the ennui, the sense of not being where one is meant to be, even the condition of the Absurd, born (as the French writer Albert Camus tells us) of the human cry confronted by the unreasonable silence of the world.

Does this refusal to underestimate the pervasiveness of human misery make his creed a pessimistic one? Many believe it does. But even while he refuses to dismiss human suffering, the Buddha's teaching, if we listen closely, is essentially a call to awakening. He neither romanticizes suffering by asking us to believe that it is ennobling, nor does he tell us that human life is only about pain. What he does point to—and even the most incorrigible optimist would have to agree with him on this—is that pleasure and pain, virtue and vice, are organically related. It is our attachment to a world that is mutable and rooted in duality that makes life deeply unsatisfying. The Buddha sums it up comprehensively: birth, decay, disease, association with the unpleasant, separation from the pleasant, not getting what we desire—all these are suffering.

Is nothing permanent? Not the self? Not even that strange, formless but reassuring inner entity we've all been told is the real thing—the soul? The Buddha doesn't answer this question directly, but draws our attention to the fact that all that we consider to be the self is, in fact, 'not-self' (anatman). This leads to the third aspect of the phenomenal world of samsara: its insubstantiality. This is often the most difficult aspect of the Buddha's teaching to accept, or even fully understand. How can the 'I' not exist? Try as I might to pretend I am a fiction, I feel too powerfully, fear too intensely, love too painfully, rage too passionately, hurt too obstinately, to believe I am a mirage.

In the tradition of the great Indian gnostics, however, Buddha would probably ask us to locate this irrepressible self and produce it before him. 'I have no peace of mind,' lamented a visitor to the great sage, Bodhidharma, who centuries later sowed the beginnings of Zen Buddhism in China. 'Bring your mind here and I will pacify it,' snapped his unsympathetic master. 'But when I seek my mind, I cannot find it,' complained the baffled student. 'There!' declared Bodhidharma. 'I have pacified your mind!' The student was apparently awakened at that very moment.

The Buddha tells us that what we consider to be the 'I'—the sense of separate selfhood or empirical individuality—is by no means real or permanent. It is an expedient invention, a convenient strategy by which we reify a fluid melange of sensations, ideas, emotions and predispositions. What makes up the psychophysical organism, the mind–body complex? Five sets of attributes (skandhas), says the Buddha. These include the body with its five senses and the mind (rupa); feelings (vedana); perceptions (samjna); disposition, intentions, mental processes (sanskara); and consciousness or the sense of separate existence (vijnana).

Each of these constituents is mutable, and the empirical self is no more than an unceasing flow of mental states and events. The 'self' then, like the word 'chariot', describes a collection of constituents in a particular relationship with one another. But no part can be isolated and regarded as the basic essence of the self or the chariot. How can we ever find the essence of the moon-in-the-water, asks the Zen Buddhist, in the famous mystical image that evokes the inseparability of subject and object. And so the Buddha invites us to accept the interpenetration of all existence and the ephemerality of the ego. 'For there is suffering,' says the Buddhist thinker, Buddhaghosha, 'but none who suffers;/ Doing exists although there is no doer;/ Extinction is but no extinguished person;/ Although there is a path, there is no goer.'

Despite his rigorous interrogation of the nature of the self, the Buddha did not dispense with the ancient law of karma and rebirth. When he drew a wheel on the ground before his first sermon in Rishipatana, he was invoking the age-old symbol of birth and rebirth, kept in motion by the human craving for sentience. Karma—the law of ethical conditionalism, of cause and effect—is the mechanism that keeps the wheel turning, that keeps us bound to birth after birth, to the cycle of recurrent becoming and dissolution. This the Buddha regarded as a natural law, psychologically valid, unfalteringly democratic. For as long as there is a desire for life as we know it, there will be life as we know it.

The Buddha deepened the traditional notion of karma, however, by asserting that it is intention, not deed that creates fresh karma. Thus, as long as we crave sentience we have it. But craving is not free choice. It is compulsion. And so it is our own inner compulsions that chain us to the cycle of birth, death and rebirth. Karma, in this scheme of things, is not a vindictive nemesis or a comforting moral rationale in an inhospitable world. Karma for the Buddha is simply a logical organic law in which the victim is as much the perpetrator, the tenant as much the architect. The hut burns, but the culprit responsible for setting it ablaze is none other than the builder, landlord and resident.

But what keeps the wheel turning? The Buddha offers the principle of Dependent Origination (pratityasamutpada) to illustrate the mechanism. He doesn't posit a series of cause and effect to explain the machinations of samsara, but simply offers a nexus of conditions. None of the twelve nidanas or components of the wheel is the first or final cause; they are merely conditions responsible for the phenomenal world and its ceaseless turning. Ignorance (avidya), says the

Buddha, is one inescapable factor of conditioned reality. From ignorance spring intentions (sanskara), which shape consciousness (vijnana). In order to individuate itself, consciousness needs a psychophysical vehicle or ego-self (nama-rupa). The ego makes use of the six organs (shadayatana: the five senses and the mind) to come into contact (sparsha) with an external reality. This gives rise to that messy welter of feelings and sensations (vedana) with which every human being is only too familiar. Feelings evoke a thirst or a desire (trishna) for the corporeal, which leads inevitably to attachment or grasping (upadana). The impulse to grasp and acquire produces another 'becoming' (bhava) which means the growth of yet another foetus in a womb. Then follows birth (jati), on which are predictably attendant old age, grief, despair and dissolution (jara-marana). Since delusion has not been snuffed out, death does not mean the end of suffering. It leads once again to intentions, and thus the cycle of suffering and rebirth endlessly perpetuates itself. Hence, the wry old Buddhist maxim: 'The cause of death is not disease, but birth.'

All of this, of course, begs the question: If there is no immortal essence to the self, then who is the serial adventurer that journeys from one birth to another? If no individual soul survives the body, then who suffers the karmic debts incurred in a previous life? The Buddhist would use the metaphor of the candle to make the point: when one candle is lit from another, the second flame is different from the first, and yet not entirely. Like a heap of dice piled on top of one another, our various births are distinct from each other, and yet linked with and supported by the previous ones. The Buddhist thinker Buddhaghosha, in the fifth century CE, offered the analogy of sour cream, that is neither entirely the same, nor wholly different from the milk that precedes it. The Buddhist monk, Nagasena, tells King Milinda that he is neither identical nor different from the infant he was several years ago. The body dies at death, but as long as craving and delusion persist, there will be a functional continuity even through rupture.

Can the cycle of rebirth be broken? It can, and the Buddha's own life was testimony to this possibility. The only miracle that Buddhism allows, it is often said, is a change of heart. Karma, in the Buddhist understanding, is not an implacable mechanistic doctrine that denies freedom, but an assertion of autonomy and the endless power of human transformation. 'By oneself evil is done; by oneself one suffers; by oneself evil is left undone, by oneself one is purified.' Since it is the grasping proclivity of the mind that perpetuates the ego, the mind can just as logically liberate itself by changing its habitual patterns and intentions. No divine intervention is required to make this miracle happen.

How then do we free ourselves? Simply by breaking

the conditional conspiracy of nidanas, rousing ourselves from millennia of self-delusion and seeing the petty self-aggrandizing charade of the ego for what it really is: a quest for personal immortality. The liberated being is the one who has seen through these narcissistic games of self-hypnosis, and destroyed the basis of the ego. 'Whatever deed, Monks, is done without greed, hatred or delusion, … that deed is annulled, cut off at the root, made like an uprooted palm-tree…, and not subject in future to the law of becoming.' In the midst of endless habitual motion, the liberated being has reached the still centre by waking up and becoming aware. The hub of the wheel is simply the knowing. Or as the *Lankavatara Sutra* puts it: the crux is 'the turning around in the seat of consciousness'.

'What is the Buddha?' asked a student. Pat came the Zen master's answer: 'The cypress tree in the courtyard!' This inimitable Zen story that reminds us yet again that the 'turning around' is often about being able to see through the subtle self-deceptions of a world where even spiritual quest can give rise to its own brand of posturing. The 'turning around' is about consciously abandoning the habitual intellectual fig leaves—of consistent theory, unassailable argument and comforting self-definition—by which we conceal our own reality from ourselves. 'Nothing is left to you at this moment,' says the Zen master, 'but to have a good laugh.'

The core of the teaching is distilled in a celebrated series of four statements that reveal the Buddha in his avatar of Master Physician (a role he clearly preferred to that of metaphysician). The result is the Four Noble Truths first propounded in the sermon at Rishipatana. The First Truth is a diagnosis: it asserts the universal human malaise of suffering. The Second Truth identifies the cause: desire, craving, thirst. The Third Truth declares that the cure must logically be the removal of the cause, which is craving. The Fourth Truth shows how the cure may be effected: through the practice of the Noble Eightfold Path (aryashtangikamarga). The basic teaching, then, is simply this: We suffer; we suffer because we are grasping, needy, self-seeking, clinging; this egocentrism can be identified and rejected; and this can be achieved through the Eightfold Path.

The Eightfold Path is not a prophet's list of oracular commandments. It is much more a physician's series of rational, non-sectarian guidelines for a life of dignity and meaning, one that awakens us to our true nature. The ethical life it advocates is consonant with the Buddha's analysis of human psychology, which explains why some contemporary Buddhists see it more as therapy than doctrine. It doesn't entail a denial, as much as a cultivation of certain aspects of the empirical self, in order to lead to a realization of its essentially fugitive nature. These are: 1. Right View/ Understanding, 2. Right

Aspiration/Motive, 3. Right Speech, 4. Right Conduct, 5. Right Livelihood, 6. Right Effort, 7. Right Mindfulness, 8. Right Concentration/Meditation. The first two factors are clearly intellectual and volitional; the next three are concerned with moral living; and the last three are concerned with the contemplative life as a means of cultivating unconditioned awareness, wisdom or prajna. And so the cognitive, the ethical and the existential blend seamlessly together to offer a timeless paradigm for integrated living, relevant across cultural and historical contexts.

The Way of the Buddha is often formulated in terms of the triple training (trishiksha) in morality (shila), meditation (samadhi) and wisdom (prajna). The training in morality encompasses a forbidding array of precepts—to avoid the taking of life, to abstain from sexual misconduct, dishonesty, harsh speech, slander, frivolity, intoxicants, covetousness, malevolence and so on. However, these undertakings are more in the nature of moral principles rather than edicts. They are also, in terms of Buddhist psychology, resolves that promote wholesome mental states, or psychic integration, which, in turn, is conducive to good karma.

However, it is meditation, or samadhi, that is considered to be 'the heart and centre of the Buddhist spiritual life', particularly in view of the Tathagata's persistent emphasis on practice over metaphysical conjecture. This direct approach to the transformation of consciousness encompasses several meditation practices, such as the remembrances of the Buddha, the Dharma and the Sangha, reflections on the body and its stages of decomposition, contemplation on death and the composition of the elements. The best-known techniques are the cultivation of loving–kindness towards all beings and the mindfulness of the breath as the bridge between the outer and inner worlds. The meditations leading to tranquil states are termed the samata meditations, while the vipasyana practices or insight meditations involve the practice of self-observation to penetrate the nature of existence.

Significantly, the Buddha does not sideline the role of the intellect or demand blind faith from the seeker. Buddhist thought describes three graded levels of understanding that broadly seem to correspond to the distinction between information, knowledge and wisdom. The first stage is the understanding that is the result of hearing (shrutamayi prajna); the second is understanding through cognition (chintamayi prajna); and the loftiest stage is wisdom through experience (bhavanamayi prajna). Intellectual understanding is superior to passive trust, but even this has its limitations. Supreme is experiential knowledge, a complete internalization of the idea, when metaphysics has become part of the marrow, understanding a matter of the gut.

What keeps us from this experiential wisdom? Why should the knowledge of our deepest selves entail such a tortuous process of quest? Ten fetters, in the Buddhist view, keep us from seeing things as they really are: a deluded belief in a separate selfhood; scepticism or doubt; a belief in rules and rituals for their own sake; sexual indulgence; ill-will; desire for existence in the world of form; desire for existence in the formless realm (a discerning insight into the nuances of human psychology); spiritual arrogance; restlessness; and ignorance. The weakening of these fetters is a sign of progress on the spiritual journey. There are varying levels of attainment. The stream entrant is one who is free of the first three fetters, and has only seven rebirths in the human or divine realms before emancipation; the once-returner has weakened the fourth and fifth fetters and will be born just once before emancipation; the non-returner has broken the first five fetters and will be reborn in a divine realm from where he will gain liberation; and finally, the enlightened one or arhant is the great victor who has broken all ten fetters and attained nirvana.

And what exactly is 'nirvana'? How do we understand that mysterious term that seems to pervade the lexicon of laymen, godmen and admen, all across the globe? It is, quite simply, the result of the unmaking of the self, the dismantling of the seductive self-perpetuating mechanism of the ego. Literally 'blowing out', it refers to the cessation of the unconscious cycle of endless becoming. The end of the path, it is awakening, deliverance, awareness, true choice, unconditioned freedom.

The emancipated being is still in possession of the five attributes of empirical individuality after nirvana, and continues to face the challenges of phenomenal reality. (These are traditionally regarded as traces of the person's vestigial karma that has still to be worked out.) However, after his death or parinirvana, he is no longer perceivable as an independent entity. He has gone beyond the condition of existence and non-existence: 'There's no measure for him who has gone beyond/ And no word that is apt to describe him, / When the Dharmas have completely fallen away/ All paths of the language have ended.'

But what remains when the karmic carousel ceases its habitual revolution? God? The eternal self? Boundless light? The causeless cause? Consciousness without content? The eternal principle? The plenum? The void? His listeners made several attempts to draw him out on the subject. However, the Buddha refused to pander to their whims by describing the indescribable. The concept of God, he said, is unnecessary to help humanity along the path of moral and spiritual awakening. The notion of an immortal self is equally unnecessary to us in the process of unmasking the delusions of the ego-self—in fact, the self-deceiving ego might actually be strengthened by such an idea. And so, as he told the seeker Malunkyaputra, all he was prepared to discuss were those problems that had a bearing on human suffering.

Perhaps unsurprisingly, later thinkers have interpreted his non-committal stance to signify that nirvana is about annihilation, total extinction, nothingness. The Buddha's words suggest, however, that this is not the whole truth either: 'Make the self your refuge and your lamp'; and yet again, 'Monks, there is a not-born, a not-become, a not-made, a not-compounded. Monks, if that unborn, not-become, not-made, not-compounded were not, there would be no escape from this here that is born, become, made, compounded.'

And even while the concept of the 'not-born' remains a mysterious one, an old Zen poem suggests that the experience of nirvana might, in fact, actually be a pretty unfussy business:

Mount Lu in misty rain; the River Che at high tide,
When I had not been there, no rest from the pain of longing!
I went there and returned... It was nothing special:
Mount Lu in misty rain, the River Che at high tide.

Jina, the Victor

'He has completed his voyage; he has gone beyond sorrow. The fetters of life have fallen from him, and he lives in full freedom.' (Chapter 7, Dhammapada)

The Buddha's life began to draw to its close after forty-five years of active ministry. The aged Master fell seriously ill during the last rains retreat at Veluva, a southern suburb of Vaishali. The canonists tell us that he conquered his illness by a conscious exercise of will since he hadn't yet made preparations for the Great Return. When he recovered, Ananda confessed to him that he had been very anxious during the illness, but had consoled himself with the thought that the 'Blessed One would not finally attain nirvana without a pronouncement about the community of Bhikshus.'

The Buddha replied, 'But, Ananda, what does the community of Bhikshus expect of me? The Law I have taught has no secret and public versions.' He pointed out that his aged body was now like an old cart held together by straps, and was only kept functional by being bandaged up. He now made his historic pronouncement that he had no intention of appointing a successor. The Tathagata's legacy was his Dharma and this would now be the community's guide. The future leader of the sangha was the Teaching. 'So, Ananda, each of you should make himself an island, himself and no other refuge; each of you should make the Law his island, the

Law and no other refuge.'

The death of the Buddha's contemporaries—King Pasenadi, as well as his disciples, Shariputra and Maudgalyayana—no doubt alerted his Order to the imminence of his own departure. In 486 BCE, the Buddha was in Jeta's Grove in Shravasti when the news of the death of his foremost disciple, Shariputra, reached him. The death of this exemplary practitioner and teacher plunged the entire Order in gloom. Ananda was deeply upset. The Buddha, however, did not lose the opportunity to deliver a sermon on the theme of mutability: 'Monks, there is separation and parting and division from all that is dear and beloved.' He spoke once more of the importance of each being his own refuge. Later he heard that his other leading disciple, Maudgalyayana, was dead, having probably been murdered by a rival shramana group. Clearly this was as much of a blow to the Order. 'The assembly is now empty for me now that Shariputra and Maudgalyayana have finally attained nirvana,' admitted the Master. He added, however, that since his great disciples had attained the final deliverance, he refused to lament.

The Master had no reservations about the Order's understanding of the Dharma. When Ananda once told him of the wrangling between other sects after the death of their spiritual leaders, the Buddha was confident that his own community would be free of such factionalism.

He pointed out that there were no two bhikshus who described the Four Noble Truths and the Eightfold Path differently. 'Dispute over livelihood or over the Code of Rules is trifling, Ananda, but should disputes arise in the community about the Path or the Way of Practice, disputes such as those would indeed be for the misfortune and unhappiness of many.'

If age had dimmed some of the creative passion of the Buddha's teaching, it was unable to cloud its clarity. When a former monk, Sunakhatta, once the Master's personal attendant, left the Order and denounced him in public, the ageing Master uttered his Lion's Roar, proclaiming to all the integrity of his practice and the perfection of his awakening. 'Even if you have to carry me about on a bed, there will still be no change in the lucidity of the Perfect One's understanding.'

One morning in Vaishali, the Buddha mentioned to Ananda that he could, if necessary, defer his death for the welfare of the community. Not listening closely, Ananda did not press the Master to do so. After Ananda's departure, the Buddha took an oath that he would make 'the final crossing' three months later. When he later disclosed this to Ananda, his attendant was perturbed and implored him to revoke his decision. However, the Master told him that it was too late. He spent the next three months continuing slowly with his travels and preparing the community for his final journey.

The Master's final meal was at the home of Chunda, the goldsmith, in Pava. The content of the meal, some believe, was pork, while others hold that it was a variety of mushroom. Unwilling to offend his host, the Buddha asked Chunda to serve him the dish, but instructed that it not be served to his monks since they would be unable to digest it. It was this act of courtesy that became the cause of the Buddha's final illness. He promptly fell ill with severe dysentery, but continued his journey towards Kushinara where he finally collapsed in a grove of sal trees. In the midst of extreme exhaustion and thirst, the Master retained total clarity of perception. He first instructed Ananda that Chunda should not be reproached as the cause of his last illness. He then gave him directions of how his body was to be disposed. He emphasized that the monks should not bother with elaborate funeral arrangements but should devote themselves to the more pressing ideal of their own emancipation.

A personal moment in the account relates how Ananda briefly left his Master's sickroom for a quiet moment of grief. He leaned his head against a door outside and wept bitter tears over the Buddha's impending death, as well as his own dread of abandonment and lack of spiritual readiness. When the Buddha heard of this, he sent for his devoted attendant and consoled him: 'Have I not repeatedly told you that there is separation and partition and division from all that is dear and beloved?' He also assured him that his long years of proximity and service to his Master had earned him considerable merit. 'Make the effort and you will soon be free of taints.'

Making desperate efforts to change the inexorable course of events, Ananda entreated him not to embark on his final journey in a small town like Kushinara when there were worthier sites like Rajagriha, Shravasti, Kosambi and Varanasi for the Great Passing. The Buddha asserted that Kushinara was no less worthy than these historic cities. He then sent Ananda to tell the residents of the town that they could come and pay their last respects, if they desired. The citizens poured in all day and the exhausted sage received them all. The last to be ordained in the sangha in the Buddha's lifetime was Subhadra, a shramana from another sect, whom the Buddha instructed Ananda to initiate that evening.

The last hours were devoted to injunctions, reminders and reiterations. The Buddha impressed upon Ananda once more the vital role of the Dharma in guiding and shaping the future of the Order: 'Ananda, it might be that some of you think: "The Master's instruction has vanished, now we have no Master!" It should not be seen like this, Ananda. What I have taught and explained to you as Dharma and Vinaya will, at my passing, be your Master.' He then summoned all his monks and asked to make use of the last opportunity to air any residual doubts about the teaching. There was silence. 'If you are unwilling to speak out of respect for me,' said the still-compassionate dying Master, 'you may consult your brethren.' He turned to Ananda and declared that there was not a single monk in the assembly who had a doubt about the Law, and even the most immature was a Stream Entrant, assured of eventual enlightenment. He turned to his assembly for the last time: 'All elements of personality are subject to decay. Strive on untiringly.'

These were the Buddha's last words. He entered the higher meditative states and finally abandoned the body, reaching the exalted state of parinirvana or perennial freedom. He was eighty and the year was probably 483 BCE. As his community of monks tried to come to terms with his departure, the tradition tells us that the natural world fittingly participated in the rites of obeisance, acknowledging the end of a major chapter in the history of man. The earth trembled, the stars blazed, the sky exploded into flame and the air was filled with the strains of an unearthly music. In the words of the *Sutra Nipata*: 'As a flame when blown out by the power of the wind/ Goes to rest and eludes definition,/ So a sage who is freed of Body-and-Name/ Goes to rest and is lost to cognisance.'

The Buddha's body lay in state for a week to enable the Mallas of Kushinara to venerate it, which they did with much fervour, accompanied by music, incense and flowers. Finally, at the advice of Anuruddha, a senior monk (also the Buddha's cousin), the body was carried to a shrine at the east end of the city, and cremated. The relics were distributed among various groups: the Mallas of Kushinara, King Ajatashatru of Magadha, the Lichhavis of Vaishali, the Shakyans of Kapilavastu, the Bulis of Allakappa, the Koliyas of Ramagama, a Brahmin from Vethadipa, and the Mallas of Pava.

Though 'the lamp of wisdom had been blown out by the wind of impermanence', the Buddha left behind a community of practitioners and a teaching that gathered enough momentum to attain the status of a world religion. The Sangha is considered, in fact, to be the oldest surviving religious order in the world, with the possible exception of its Jain counterpart. The teachings of the Buddha has since diversified, undergone numerous transformations, faced several challenges, but has continued to derive its identity from certain essential tenets discovered and articulated by Siddhartha Gautama more than two millennia ago.

From Death to Immortality

The need to systematize the doctrine for the sake of posterity was felt immediately after the Buddha's death. Mahakashyapa, the veteran monk, could not forget an incident that occurred on his way to Kushinara from Pava. On hearing that the Shakyan Sage had attained parinirvana, a monk in Mahakashyapa's entourage was heard to exult: 'Enough, brothers, do not weep and wail! We are well rid of the Great Shramana. We were always bothered by his saying: "You are allowed to do this, you are not allowed to do that!" Now we can do what we like and not do what we don't like!' These lines stayed with Mahakashyapa as a reminder of how the Master's teaching could be distorted after his time in the absence of a formal consensus on the doctrine. He proposed that the senior monks convene and rehearse the Law and the Discipline together 'so that no wrong teachings or rules creep in, and no heretics become strong while the experts become feeble'.

During the rains of 483 BCE, five hundred monks assembled at Rajagriha for what was to become the first Buddhist council. All the monks were apparently arhants, except for Ananda, who was included because of his long years of association with the Buddha. The canon offers us a comforting account of how Ananda became an arhant the night before the synod convened. Embarrassed at being the odd man out in an assembly of the spiritual cognoscenti, Ananda spent the night contemplating the mutability of the body. At a dramatic moment before he went to sleep, just 'before his head touched the pillow and after his feet left the ground' his heart was liberated from the shadow of delusion. He now attained the state that had eluded him for forty-four years of monastic life.

In the following seven months, Upali, the former barber, was appointed the expert on Vinaya, or matters of discipline, and Ananda the authority on Dharma or doctrine. This marked the beginning of two principal 'baskets' of the Buddhist canon: the *Vinaya Pitaka* and the *Sutra Pitaka*. The assembly was free to object, add, clarify or modify any of their statements before they were decreed canonical and committed to memory.

The impulse to codify and interpret the Buddha's doctrine gained momentum over time. A hundred years later, a second council was held in Vaishali in 383 BCE in order to debate the relevance of certain rules of discipline. Those in favour of strict adherence to the old monastic rules considered themselves the supporters of the Doctrine of the Elders, while the Mahasanghikas, the unorthodox voices who endorsed a certain flexibility and sympathy to the needs of the laity, seceded and held a council of their own. This signified the start of a dichotomy within Buddhism that was later to develop into a distinction between Theravada and Mahayana. It is believed that the result of the second council was the modification and expansion of the canon in consonance with the growing impulse to venerate the Buddha as a divine being rather than a human figure.

A third council was convened in Pataliputra in 253 BCE under the aegis of Ashoka Maurya, the renowned emperor whose horror at the excesses of war converted him from pursuing a nakedly expansionist policy to an evangelical Buddhist mission of peace and brotherhood. A thousand monks, under the leadership of Ashoka's preceptor, Maudgalyaputra Tishya, reviewed the canon over a period of nine months, making several revisions and interpolations. A third scholastic work called the *Abhidharma* was now added to the *Vinaya* and *Sutra* Pitakas. It was during the reign of Ashoka that missionaries were encouraged to carry the teaching of the Buddha to different parts of the ancient world, including Ceylon, Burma, Syria, Egypt, Cyrene, Epirus and Macedonia.

It was more than three centuries later that the emperor Kanishka (78–101 CE) convened a fourth council. This was attended by five hundred monks, chiefly Theravadins from India, Tibet and China, and presided over by Vasumitra. By the first century CE, the Mahayana strand of Buddhism had emerged, the image of the Buddha had begun to gain currency (marking the first anthropomorphic representation of the Buddha who had earlier been represented only by sacred symbols), and the first Buddhist scriptures had been written down in Ceylon. These came to be named the Tripitaka or Three Baskets since they were originally written on palm leaves and preserved in baskets.

Thus, the Buddhist canon came into being as 'a series of deposits from the oral tradition', the more esoteric among the scriptures supposedly being committed to the written word later than the exoteric. The Tripitaka consists of three parts: the *Vinaya Pitaka* (Basket of Order) that deals with the organization and code of conduct for the monks; the *Sutra Pitaka* (Basket of Discourses) that contains sections called the Agamas or Nikayas which deal with the dialogues and sermons of the Buddha (with varying numbers in the Theravada and Mahayana traditions); and the *Abhidharma Pitaka* (Basket of Higher Teaching) that consists of scholastic treatises which concern themselves with specialized metaphysical discourse. The famous Dhammapada or the Footprints of the Law is part of the *Sutra Pitaka*. The Buddhist canon also includes the Tantras, esoteric texts that deal with ritual and yoga as a means of attaining liberation.

The Buddha's endorsement of the demotic idiom over the mandarin, and the fact that his teaching was orally transmitted for two or three centuries and sometimes longer, accounts for the absence of any one canonical language in Buddhism. Different Buddhist schools seem to have had canons in Prakrit, Paishachi, Apabhramsha and Sanskrit. The Pali canon, written in Ceylon (Sri Lanka), is often accorded a more definitive status, but according to some scholars, this is simply because of the 'historical accident' of it being the Indian scripture to have survived in its entirety in the original language.

As Buddhist teaching gained influence and patronage, the monastery became a vital nucleus of intellectual and artistic life. Monasteries such as Ajanta in west India, Anuradhapura in Ceylon, and vibrant cosmopolitan universities such as Nalanda in east India and Taxila in the north-west, flourished between the first and seventh centuries. In this era of buoyant expansion, Buddhism spread as far as China, Korea, Japan and the Pacific Islands.

The oeuvre of Buddhist discourse was enriched and expanded by the contributions of several great monks, scholars and mystics. The non-canonical Pali work, 'Milindapanha' or 'Questions of King Milinda', the famous lively dialogue between Buddhist monk Nagasena and the Indo-Greek king Menander (who ruled over north-western India in the second century BCE), consists of 304 questions and answers on different aspects of Buddhism. Buddhaghosha, a great Pali scholar and commentator of the fifth century CE, travelled to Ceylon during the reign of King Mahanama where he compiled a compendium of the Tripitaka called the 'Visuddhimagga' or the 'Path of Purification', and wrote and translated several Sinhalese commentaries. There were also important commentaries written by the Pali scholars, Buddhadatta and Dhammapala in the fifth and sixth centuries CE respectively.

As Buddhism spread, Sanskrit gradually began to gain ascendancy over the vernacular. Asvaghosha, the great Sanskrit poet and dramatist of the first century CE and Kalidasa's illustrious precursor, wrote important poetic works like the *Buddhacharita* and *Saundarananda*. A vital contribution was the Madhyamika school of philosophy propounded by Nagarjuna in the second century CE. Propagating the teachings of the *Prajnaparamita*, the great Mahayana sutra, this original scholar and mystic advocated a Middle Path between existence and non-existence, self and non-self, reality and unreality, asserting that there is no real difference between samsara and nirvana because all is sunyata—'of a non-essential and indefinable character, and void in essence'. Asanga and Vasubandhu, two brothers and great Buddhist monk–scholars of the fourth century, Dignaga, the founder of Buddhist logic in the seventh century, and Dharmakirti, another logician of the same century, among several others, made significant intellectual contributions. Outstanding missionaries like Mahindra (who took Buddhism to Ceylon during Ashoka's reign in the third century BCE), Kumarajiva (who went to China in 383 BCE), Paramartha and Bodhidharma (both of whom travelled to China in the sixth century CE) became conduits and interpreters of the Buddhist teachings in other parts of the world. Gradually, the seminal insights of Siddhartha Gautama grew over the centuries into a rich and flourishing tradition of accumulated wisdom, evolving without the fear of persecution.

By the seventh century, however, Buddhism in India was on the decline. How does one explain the gradual atrophy of this vigorous spiritual culture? Several reasons have been offered, but most scholars concede that the phenomenon still remains something of a mystery. The absence of sustained patronage, the tenacity of the caste system, the resurgence of Brahminism, the growing economic security of the monasteries (that possibly eroded grass-roots contact with the laity), are some of the probable factors accounting for its state of near-total oblivion by the eleventh century. The advent of the Muslim invaders was the last nail in the coffin.

The lasting and beneficial impact of Buddhism on various forms of Hindu thought and practice, however, remains undeniable. As scholar Bhikshu Sangharakshita (in A.L. Basham's *Cultural History of India*) puts it: 'While Buddhism put some of its new wine into the old bottles, Hinduism redesigned its bottles the better to accommodate and preserve the new wine. The result was that if Buddhism appropriated the forms of

Hinduism, Hinduism assimilated something of the spirit of Buddhism.'

The Wheel Rolls On

Today, like any living faith, Buddhism has mutated into dynamic and distinct forms in various cultures of the globe—ranging from Vajrayana in Tibet to Theravada in Sri Lanka and Myanmar, from Zen in China to the Pure Land schools of Japan and Dalit Neo-Buddhism in India. The distinction between Theravada and Mahayana has been variously described over the years, from Heinrich Zimmer's 'Little Ferryboat' and 'Large Ferryboat' image to Christmas Humphrey's metaphor of the wheel where Theravada is the hub and Mahayana the spokes. While Theravada stresses the importance of rigorous practice of a moral and contemplative life as the means to reach Buddhahood, Mahayana seems to regard Buddhahood as something innate, to be tapped more intuitively. If Theravada regards it as something to be attained, Mahayana sees it as something to be discovered; for the former, nirvana is a challenging future goal, for the latter, it is an ever-present reality.

Theravada underscores the prajna or wisdom aspect of the Buddha's teaching, while Mahayana also highlights karuna or compassion. Or again, at the risk of generalization, Theravada sees the Eightfold Path as the means to an end; Mahayana refuses to distinguish between the two. A Zen master puts it succinctly: Theravada represents the humanity of the Buddha, while Mahayana accentuates the Buddha nature of humanity.

The Theravadin ideal is embodied in the Sanskrit term arhant, which denotes a follower of the Buddha who has gained insight into the true nature of things by sheer perseverance and diligent application. The Mahayana ideal, on the other hand, is the bodhisattva, who undertakes responsibility not only for his own salvation, but that of all sentient beings. Having attained nirvana, he does not cleave to samsara or shun it, but simply defers his own release from the phenomenal world in order to help others on the path to deliverance. The arhant ideal draws inspiration from the Buddha's repeated injunction to his followers to act as lights unto themselves, to make themselves and the Law their only refuge. The bodhisattva ideal, on the other hand, seems to find its inspiration in the Buddha's pivotal decision to return to minister to a suffering world, rather than remain in a life of detached contemplation. None of these forms validate any sacred scripture or godhead however, despite the more theist inclination in some forms of Mahayana.

The number of Buddhist adherents in the world is often difficult to determine because of the fact that Buddhism has entered into alliances or been amalgamated with other faiths and liberation ideologies. Broadly speaking, Theravada Buddhism (or what is known as the Southern School) flourishes today in countries of Southeast Asia, such as Sri Lanka, Thailand, Myanmar, Laos, Kampuchea and other regions of the Far East, while Mahayana (or the Northern School) is dominant in China, Korea, Japan, Tibet, Nepal, Sikkim, Bhutan, Ladakh, Mongolia and Vietnam.

Buddhism reached America in the late nineteenth century, in the form of the Mahayana movements carried by Japanese and Chinese immigrants, and probably received a fillip with the establishment of the Theosophical Society in New York in 1875. In Europe, the philosophical contribution of Schopenhauer, Edwin Arnold's influential *Light of Asia* and the work of other scholars and artists established the Buddhist presence in the nineteenth century. Today, the West is witnessing an unprecedented Buddhist revival with new educational and meditation centres of varied affiliations opening every year. Inevitably, an integrated and mature Buddhism coexists with the more faddish variety that represents the 'aloha-amigo' or 'salad-bar' brand of cosmetic spiritual eclecticism.

As the place where it all began, India continues to occupy a significant position in the international Buddhist landscape. Thousands of international pilgrims, eager to retrace the path of the Buddha, still frequent Bodhgaya, in modern-day Bihar, south of the river Ganga. Here stands the famous Mahabodhi temple, as well as the bodhi tree that ostensibly marks the precise spot where a young seeker reached the end of his quest. The bodhi tree is believed to be the progeny of the original tree, or of the tree in Anuradhapura in Sri Lanka (which itself was probably a sapling from the original). This is obviously not the same tree that offered sanctuary to one of history's greatest men. However, it is a close relative, and of sufficient horticultural pedigree to ensure its importance in the eyes of those who flock to this small, dusty town.

Rishipatana—or modern Sarnath in Uttar Pradesh—also continues to attract transcontinental seekers. Some ten kilometres north of Varanasi, it has several ancient ruins that suggest a flourishing monastic tradition of some vintage, as well as temples and a park to commemorate the site where the Enlightened One delivered his first awe-inspiring sermon on the 'Turning of the Wheel of the Law'. Lumbini (the Master's birth place) on the India–Nepal border, Rajgir (where he met and converted his leading disciples Shariputra and Maudgalyayana), Sanchi (which houses the largest stupa in the country) Shravasti, Nalanda, Amaravati, Nagarjunakonda, the hauntingly beautiful cave temples of Ajanta, Ellora, Kanheri and Karla in western India—all these remain vital spots on the Buddhist pilgrim's map. Questors committed to completing the Great Shramana's trail also make it a point to visit Kushinagar, south of Gorakhpur in modern Uttar Pradesh, where the Buddha's parinirvana is marked by the Makutabandhana stupa that houses some of his relics.

While there is an almost flamboyant renewal of world interest in the teachings of India's leading spiritual victor, his position in India today is often viewed as peripheral. How many locals flock to the great sites of Buddhist pilgrimage? Have these places become merely places of historical and archaeological importance to the average Indian rather than hubs of throbbing spiritual ardour? Although international pilgrims may seem to outnumber the Indian, it is clear that the Buddhist influence in India cannot be easily dismissed.

Buddhism in India has seen a gradual but unmistakable reawakening over the past two centuries, its quiet history punctuated by a couple of spectacular moments. In the mid-nineteenth century, there were individuals like Mahavir Swamy (a veteran of the First Indian War of Independence in 1857), who was ordained by a Buddhist monk in Burma, and settled down in Kushinagar. By the end of the nineteenth century, the resurgence was more marked, fuelled by the pioneering contributions of western orientalists and a growing spirit of nationalism. The year 1891 saw the establishment of the Mahabodhi Society for the promotion of Buddhism in India by Anagarika Dharmapala from Ceylon. The growing influence of the Buddhist faith was also perhaps evident in the Indian government's decision to inscribe the Ashoka Chakra on the national flag in 1947. A historic moment in post-independence Indian Buddhism was the flight of the fourteenth Dalai Lama from Tibet to India with thousands of refugees in 1959. As host to several monks and lay-members of the exiled Tibetan community, India now has the largest number of monastic and educational Tibetan Buddhist centres in the world. An even more decisive moment occurred on 14 October 1966, when Dr B.R. Ambedkar converted to Buddhism, along with half a million Dalit followers, in symbolic protest against the inequalities of the caste system. The gesture stands testimony to the way in which the emancipatory spirit of the Buddha's teaching finds new resonances in modern contexts of oppression.

And so, the Buddha lives on in the land of his birth in a million ways, both overt and subtle. The irrepressible theist impulse has ensured his appropriation (or integration, depending on one's point of view) into the fecund pantheon of Hindu deities. Thus, his benign visage is regularly enshrined in calendar art devoted to the theme of dashavatara, or the ten avatars of Vishnu, all over the country. In his Gandhara sculptural aspect, he remains the subject of the countless objets d'art that regularly grace the mantel of middle-class homes in India as all over the world. Political and spiritual leaders across the ideological spectrum routinely cite his emphasis on 'human values', 'tolerance' and 'world peace' as proof of the timeless relevance of the Buddhist gospel in a global multicultural context.

But perhaps the most important aspect of the Buddhist revival in India is the fact that the practitioners of Buddhist techniques of meditation seem to be markedly on the rise. The technique of vipassana meditation, spearheaded by S.N. Goenka (a pupil of the Buddhist teacher U Ba Khin) has its centre in Igatpuri, north of Mumbai, and several branches all over the country. Though the course is rigorous in its regimen, its refreshing absence of ritual hocus-pocus and unwavering focus on that most non-sectarian of phenomena—the human breath—attracts a growing tribe of adherents. Still others flock to Dharamsala in Himachal Pradesh towards the inspirational figure of a man who is regarded as an incarnation of the Avalokiteshwara Buddha of compassion—the simple, unaffectedly charismatic monk, statesman and spiritual leader, the Dalai Lama, whose presence has notably increased interest in Tibetan Buddhism. At a mere click of the computer mouse, a truly mind-boggling list of Dharma centres in the country unfolds before an interested seeker. These range from Tibetan Dzogchen and Rigpa centres to a New Delhi sangha devoted to

Vietnamese Zen and even a Bodhi Zendo Retreat Centre in the idyllic environs of Kodaikanal, run by a Jesuit Zen master, ordained in Japan!

It is then, perhaps, at the level of practice—invisible, plodding practice—that the wheel of Dharma set in motion all those centuries ago in a park in Rishipatana still rolls on in the land of Siddhartha Gautama's birth in its most meaningful and enduring way.

Epilogue

'Like a spider caught in its own web is a person driven by fierce cravings. Break out of the web, and turn away from the world of sensory pleasure and sorrow.'
(Chapter 24, Dhammapada)

It is not difficult to see why the Middle Path of Shakyamuni has remained relevant to a variety of seekers down the centuries. Much has been said of its non-authoritarianism, its rationality, its endorsement of the essential inseparability of the ethical and the spiritual, its unshakeable humanism, its efficacy as a therapeutic device. Above all, in the anchorless, compulsively extremist world we live in, it seems increasingly to represent a path of sanity.

The legacy of Gautama Buddha is a dharma that offers the contemporary seeker a means to negotiate a route between perennially seductive polarities: between self-denial and self-aggrandizement, chronic doubt and blind faith, cerebralism and sentimentalism, dogmatism and relativism, eternalism and nihilism, quietism and feverish engagement. This is not a path of docile compromise, a stodgy middle-of-the-road complacency, but a precarious transformational journey that involves poise without tension, a creative equilibrium between effortlessness and effort (not unlike the Taoist notion of 'wu-wei', illuminated by Lao Tzu's remark that ruling the kingdom of the self is like cooking a small fish on a fire: if one turns it too much in the pan, it will disintegrate!).

The Middle Way is centrally concerned with how to live vitally, spiritedly and intelligently in a dysfunctional world. The Buddha was a lover of peace, but his metaphors were at times startlingly martial. He asks us to become freedom fighters, not tame strategists. What he offers is not a prescription for anaesthetized pain-free living. Clearly, his own life had its fair share of mental and physical hardship even after his historic enlightenment at Bodhgaya. When he invites us to choose the Middle Path, then, he asks us to make the courageous choice to look adversity in the eye while being anchored in inner stillness, to join the stream rather than stay content with endlessly circling the goldfish bowl.

Significantly, the Middle Path does not advocate denying or escaping the phenomenal world. Instead, it allows one to be transformed by embracing the world, but without clinging to it. This path is also the goal, the journey also the destination. Contemporary scholar, peace activist and Zen master Thich Nhat Hanh puts it unforgettably: 'The secret of Buddhism is to be awake here and now. There is no way to peace; peace is the way. There is no way to enlightenment; enlightenment is the way. There is no way to liberation; liberation is the way.'

The enduring image of the Buddha as the simple

alms-gatherer with a begging bowl remains to this day a reminder that one can acknowledge one's needs without being enslaved by them. The Eightfold Path doesn't tell us to be ashamed of our desires, even while it affirms a moral life. It tells us, instead, that by becoming alert to our drives we are no longer driven by them. Or as a Western Buddhist psychotherapist says, the spirit of Buddhism 'is not about slaying the inner dragon but about riding it'. The fact that the night of the Buddha's enlightenment was also the night when he confronted some of the most tormenting fantasies and cataclysmic emotions of his lifetime is an inspiring reassurance that inner turbulence is no reason to despair.

Over the centuries, Siddhartha Gautama has turned into superman, saviour, munificent messiah for some questors. While the impulse to venerate is perhaps inevitable, it would be unfortunate to forget that Gautama Buddha started out as a layman, not a professional; a spiritual upstart, not the traditional heir. His was the approach of the unlicensed seeker as he fearlessly spread the word that the world belongs to anyone audacious enough to pursue the path of self-inquiry. His is a voice that commiserates with the dispossessed and grieving all over the world, and yet speaks with ringing joy of the universally attainable state of freedom, unconditioned by circumstance. Seeker, dissenter, mystic, surgeon, he holds out to future

generations not a revealed religion, but a dynamic and
syncretic wisdom that has spawned a tradition, both
cohesive and creative.

The affirmation of each human being as a vehicle
to his own salvation makes this unambiguously a
doctrine of empowerment. The refusal to offer any
anthropomorphic embodiment of the Ultimate also
means that there is none to fear or propitiate, and none
to hold culpable but the self. The onus of enlightenment
rests squarely on the human being. It is sometimes alleged
that the Buddhist view refuses to fulfil every seeker's
deep-seated need for the sacred. But what the Buddha
offers us, instead, is the limitless freedom of discovering
the sacred for ourselves. There is no attempt to preserve
it in theological formaldehyde. He gives us a teaching
that is to be experienced, rather than enforced. The
Buddhist teacher does no more than 'sell water by the
river', turning us from dependent consumers into
legitimate owners, telling us that what we seek to buy
is, in fact, freely available. We don't have to attain
Buddhahood, he reminds us, but simply drop our
delusions.

It is this spirit of unabashed freedom from varied
oppressive constraints, including those of hearth and
husband, that suffuses the jubilant paeans sung by the
Buddhist nuns in the Therigatha: 'So free am I, so
gloriously free,/ Free from three petty things —/ From

mortar and pestle and from my twisted lord,/ Freed from rebirth and death I am,/ And all that had held me down/ Is hurled away.' It is the same spirit that permeates the Buddhist missionary Bodhidharma's legendary reply to Emperor Wu of China when asked about the nature of the supreme truth: 'Vast emptiness, nothing holy'. It also pervades the playful irreverence of much Zen spirituality and literature, its emphasis on spontaneity, immediacy and naturalness.

The Buddha's emphasis on anitya (impermanence) and anatman (not-self) still makes many believe that this world-view leaves little room for hope or love. However, this suspicion is banished when one considers the potential for freedom implicit in the notion of change. While the loss of a permanent self is terrifying, it also signifies the end of isolation, the loss of separateness. The Buddha's penetrating insight under the bodhi tree of the interdependence of all things brings with it the implication of collective responsibility and universal connectedness—that we are all a part of a great, staggeringly complex molecular dance that knows no beginning or end. The famous Mahayana Buddhist image from Japan is that of a vast net woven with glittering multifaceted jewels. Each jewel represents an individual existence, reflecting every other jewel as well as countless reflections of itself. It is this insight of 'dependent origination' that inspires the Mahayana ideal of the bodhisattva and the Theravada meditation on maitra (loving–kindness). Modern science only confirms this when it informs us that 'a butterfly stirring the air today in Peking can transform storm systems next month in New York'.

'Seeing emptiness, have compassion,' said Milarepa, the great Tibetan mystic and hermit of the eleventh century, distilling the creative paradox central to Buddhism—the inseparability of prajna (wisdom) and karuna (compassion). The Mahayana text, *Prajnaparamita Hridaya Sutra*, offers us a harmonious resolution of these apparent opposites: 'Form is not different from emptiness; emptiness is not different from form. Form is precisely emptiness; emptiness is precisely form.' And so nirvana and samsara are not mutually exclusive. If wisdom helps us see that form is emptiness, compassion is born of the insight that emptiness is form. 'The trick,' says one Tibetan master, 'is to have positive intention during the dream. This is the essential point. This is true spirituality.'

And yet, while the phenomenal world may be unreal, it is not non-existent. The Buddha himself was only too aware of the searing presence of suffering in the world, and spent his life addressing this fundamental human problem. The difficulty of dismissing the relative world is reflected in the poignant haiku of the renowned Japanese poet Issa, written on the death of his son: 'This dewdrop world—/ It may be a dewdrop,/ And yet—and yet—.' On the other hand, engagement with the relative world is rescued from feverishness and subtle egotism by prajna or wisdom. And as the Dalai Lama pointed out recently during a talk on the suffering of the exiled Tibetan people, 'Compassion would be unbearable sometimes without the wisdom of emptiness.'

Does the Buddha's non-committal stance on transcendental realities give rise to a bleak view of life? Is the universe a grim mindless mechanism running on autopilot? No, particularly if one considers the concept of the trikaya, or three bodies, adopted by Mahayana in a later phase of Buddhism—a concept that is generous and inclusive enough to accommodate the conception of both a personal and impersonal godhead. This offers the idea of three intrinsic aspects of the self: the deepest level is the unconditioned, indestructible, deathless absolute or dharmakaya; its blissful subtle body, a spontaneous radiation of light and energy, is the sambhogakaya; and the third dimension is the nirmanakaya or gross material manifestation, born of compassionate enlightened energy (the realm in which Siddhartha Gautama and all the other historic Buddhas appeared in physical form to minister to humanity).

Besides, the Buddha's refusal to elaborate on the state of nirvana is the mark of an egalitarian mystic; it allows everyone the space to experience it in his or her own unique way. And so we have the rich welter of mysterious, contradictory utterances down the ages, at times metaphorical and suggestive, and at other times, laconic and anti-romantic, all of which point to, but never explain the ultimate state of tathata, suchness: 'It is merely the immaculate/ Looking naturally at itself.' (Nyoshul Khen Rinpoche); 'Old pond/ Leap splash/ A frog' (Basho); 'Knowing is false understanding; not knowing is blind ignorance' (Nan-ch'uan); 'basic sanity' (Chogyam Trungpa); 'A fallen flower/ Returning to the branch?/ It was a butterfly' (Moritake); 'Remember the example of an old cow/ She's content to sleep in a barn/ You have to eat, sleep and shit—/ That's unavoidable—/ Beyond that is none of your business' (Patrul Rinpoche); 'The sound of the scouring/ Of the saucepan blends/ With the tree-frogs' voices' (Ryokan); 'We eat, excrete, sleep and get up/ This is our world/ All we have to do after that—/ Is to die' (Ikkyu); 'No words can describe it/ No example can point to it/ Samsara does not make it worse/ Nirvana does not make it better' (Dudjom Rinpoche).

The legacy of the Buddha is not free of inconsistency. The image of the gun-toting Buddhist monk on the cover of a well-known magazine some years ago was a searing reminder that the most rational and gnostic of world religions is not free of violence or absolutism. Moreover, for all his revolutionary stances, the failures of the

Buddha cannot be wished away either. His radical indictment of caste clearly did not prove radical enough. The later dependence of the sangha on political patronage in all probability compromised the integrity of its position, limiting the Buddhist attack on caste to the ideological rather than the material sphere. The institutionalization of the sangha also spelt its own share of internal contradictions. If the ideal was a community of committed wayfarers, the peril of spiritual complacency, infighting and factionalism remained a perennial challenge that was frequently impossible to resist (as the Buddha realized with growing disenchantment in his own lifetime).

But there is no denying that what threatens Buddhism from without is far more disturbing today than what undermines it from within. The desecration of the Bamiyan Buddha, witnessed in mute horror by the entire world on its television sets, represents one of the most pervasive forms of violence in the world today. And yet, every act of violation, as the Buddha would himself have observed, is preceded by an act of inner vandalism. As long as a turbulent interiority remains unhealed, there can be no escape from the unrelenting historical catalogue of human violence in different parts of the world—the endless replay of man's need to crush, silence, obliterate and erase all that seems fearful and alien. In contemporary India, where the richly heterodox tradition of the Hindu faith seems increasingly to be defined by a tribe of sentries rather than seekers, the Buddha's message of rationality, self-determination and the Middle Way takes on an altogether new urgency.

More personally, I find that revisiting literature on the Buddha doesn't make any of the age-old questions— about life, death, suffering and the contaminated, embattled ego-self—go away. If anything, they become sharper, edgier, more focussed. But only for a while. Gradually, even if the answers don't seem forthcoming, the space around the questions grows just a little larger, just a little emptier. And strangely enough, there is comfort in that spaciousness, a brief sense of sanctuary in that silence. And at such times, one begins to gain a flickering insight into what it takes to be a traveller walking the path of Shakyamuni.

On seeing the great stone sculptures of the Buddha in Sri Lanka, the Trappist scholar and monk, Thomas Merton, summed up the challenge that the Buddha continues to represent to a humanity that both craves and fears an unmoored freedom: 'Filled with every possibility, questioning nothing, knowing everything, rejecting nothing, the peace not of emotional resignation but of Madhyamika, of sunyata, that has seen through every question without trying to discredit anyone or anything—without refutation—without establishing some other argument. For the doctrinaire, the mind that needs well-established positions, such peace, such silence can be frightening.'

If the smile of the Buddha is born of compassion, his sometimes forbidding silence is born of prajna, the beatitude that is the reward of only those who dare to discard ancient carapaces of self-deception—those who dare to leave the burning house in the conviction that houses are unnecessary to be at home in the world.

Bibliography

Ahir, D.C., *Heritage of Buddhism*, B.R. Publishing Corporation, Division of DK Publishers and Distributors Pvt. Ltd., 1989.

Armstrong, Karen, *Buddha*, Orion Books, 2002.

Basham, A.L. (ed), *A Cultural History of India*, Oxford University Press, 1975.

Brazier, David, *The Feeling Buddha: A Buddhist Psychology of Character, Adversity and Passion*, HarperCollins India, 1999.

Burnson, Matthew E., *The Dalai Lama's Book of Wisdom*, Random House, 1997.

Conze, Edward (trans), *Buddhist Scriptures*, Penguin, 1959.

Coomaraswamy, A.K., and Horner, I.B., *Gotama the Buddha*, Rupa and Co., 2003.

Easwaran, Eknath (trans), *The Dhammapada*, Penguin, 1996.

Harvey, Andrew, *Essential Teachings: His Holiness the Dalai Lama*, Rupa and Co., 1996.

Humphreys, Christmas, *Buddhism: An Introduction and Guide*, Penguin Books, 1951.

Kuppuram, G., and Kumudmani, K. (ed), *Buddhist*

Heritage in India and Abroad, Sundeep Prakashan, New Delhi, 1992.

Mishra, Pankaj, *An End to Suffering—The Buddha In The World*, Picador, 2004.

Nanamoli, Bhikkhu, *The Life of the Buddha*, Buddhist Publication Society, Kandy, Sri Lanka, 1978.

Radhakrishnan, *Indian Philosophy*, Vol 1, Unwin Brothers Ltd., 1929.

Ramesan, N., *Glimpses of Buddhism*, The Government of Andhra Pradesh, 1961.

Rhys Davids, T.W. (trans), *Buddhist Birth Stories: Jataka Tales*, Routledge, 1925.

Rinpoche, Sogyal, *The Tibetan Book of Living and Dying*, Rupa and Co., 1993.

Rockhill, Woodville V. (trans), *The Life of the Buddha and the Early History of his Order*, Navrang, New Delhi, 1991.

Schumann, H.W., *The Historical Buddha*, Arkana, Penguin, 1989.

Singh, Iqbal, *Gautama Buddha*, Oxford University Press, 1994.

Skilton, Andrew, *A Concise History of Buddhism*, Windhorse Publications, 1994.

Tharu, Susie and Lalita, K. (ed) *Women Writing in India*, Pandora Press, HarperCollins, 1991.

Thich Nhat Hanh, *Interbeing*, Full Circle, New Delhi, India, 1997.

Watts, Alan, *The Way of Zen*, Vintage Books, 1957.

Wilson Ross, Nancy, *Buddhism: A Way of Life and Thought*, Vintage Books, Random House, 1981.

Yoshinori, Takeuchi (ed), *Buddhist Spirituality: Indian, Southeast Asian, Tibetan and Early Chinese*, The Crossword Publishing Company, New York.